Unsingle

The art and science of finding true love

Written and illustrated by
Louise Gabriel

FINCH PUBLISHING
SYDNEY

Unsingle: The art and science of finding true love

First published in 2014 in Australia and New Zealand by Finch Publishing Pty Limited, ABN 49 057 285 248, Suite 2207, 4 Daydream Street, Warriewood, NSW, 2102, Australia.

14   8 7 6 5 4 3 2 1

There is a National Library of Australia Cataloguing-in-Publication entry available at the National Library.

Edited by Karen Gee
Editorial assistance by Peter King
Text typeset by Jo Hunt
Illustrations by Louise Gabriel
Cover design by Ingrid Kwong
Printed by Griffin Press

The paper used to produce this book is a natural, recyclable product made from wood grown in sustainable plantation forests. The manufacturing processes conform to the environmental regulations in the country of origin.

Finch titles can be viewed and purchased at **www.finch.com.au**

Contents

For my beloved husband

The beginning

If you're single and you don't want to be, there is a fairly simple explanation. Whether or not you have had relationships in the past, your singleness is not caused by anything outside yourself. It's because you're not playing for Team Love.

If this statement has you scratching your head, bear with me. It will be worth it.

How *Unsingle* came to be

My life was good, except for the fact that I didn't have someone to share it with. I had great friends, I'd travelled, and had bought myself a nice little place in a great location. I was working in a bookshop I loved, which specialised in personal and professional development. The books I read, the people I met there and the ideas I was exposed to gave me plenty of food for thought regarding my relationship status. But nothing was clicking. My friends were mystified by my ongoing singleness, as was I. I didn't understand it at all. So I enjoyed their company and my new home, all the while wondering why I was still single. What was going on?

Then something new emerged: a documentary-style movie that explained the newest scientific breakthrough when it came to the human mind. It seemed my brain was constantly changing and rewiring with regard to what I thought about and gave my focused attention to. What I focused on and gave my attention to shaped my brain and subsequently my life and my relationships. It was called 'neuroplasticity'.

Even for someone like me, who was exposed to the latest theories and concepts through my work on a regular basis, I knew this was different. Sitting in the cinema watching the movie with friends, my mind was spinning with implications. A scene about a woman whose belief was that love never worked out for her had me sitting forward in my seat. There was an animation of her neural pathways and her cute little love neurons being bombarded by her negative thoughts, eventually surrendering and being destroyed. I immediately wondered how my love neurons were doing. The wheels started turning, but I had yet to connect the dots.

A month or so later, I was on my lunch break one day. Walking back to work with my sushi in my hand I passed the newsagency and reached for a magazine to browse while I was eating. About to hand over my money, I glanced at the headline announcing the latest marriage meltdown and experienced the ultimate light-bulb moment. *This* was what I was giving my focused attention to? *This* was the diet I was feeding my sweet little love neurons? Reading this stuff was focusing on everything I didn't want. I realised there and then that the only thing standing between true love and me – was me.

The next couple of weeks were a revelation. I started to take note of what I thought about, my off-the-cuff comments, where I directed my energy and my focus. What I discovered pulled me up up short. Much as I wanted my own happily ever after, thought about it, pined for it and fervently wished for it, I spent a significant amount of time focusing my attention on love not working out. I listened to friends talk about problems with their partners and thought that was all there was to their relationship. I watched entertainment news shows that reported the marriage woes of any celeb who drew breath. I zeroed in on stories that focused on romance being a risky business or on the joys of being single.

No wonder I was stuck. I was cancelling myself out. My **love** neurons didn't stand a chance. Sure I spent time thinking about how much I wanted love but I spent more time thinking about the woes of love, and I'd been doing it for years. Wow! The things I'd done in the beginning to make me feel better about my single status, beliefs that had initially given me solace, were reinforcing my solitude and holding me there. What it came down to was, at some point I'd tipped my internal balance and all of my focus onto being and feeling single. My predominant thoughts about relationships were either negative or fearful. The love zone of my brain was not in great shape, a fact that, up until now, I'd been completely oblivious to.

I was most definitely not playing for Team Love.

Are you playing for Team Love?

'OMG there's a Team Love? Where do I sign up?' If you're not playing for Team Love there is an invisible barrier standing between you and the relationship of your dreams. This barrier is made up of the negative conscious – and subconscious thoughts and beliefs you have about sharing your life with someone. And if you want to unsingle yourself, those beliefs need to change. How? **By flipping the switch on your thoughts, turning down the volume on the negative and amping up the positive love input in your life.**

Ten signs you're not playing for Team Love

'Negative about love? Who? Me?' Think this doesn't apply to you and that you're super positive about love and matters of the heart? You might be surprised.

1. You've wanted a serious relationship for a while now and it hasn't materialised.
2. You hear about a celeb love scandal and immediately jump online to read every detail. You follow it. You talk about it. You almost take it personally and think about how you would feel if it was you.
3. Someone you know breaks up on Facebook and you want to know all the specifics. It makes you feel better about being single or about your own relationship woes.
4. You're drawn to books, articles, movies, programs and songs that focus on train crash relationships, or on being alone, lonely, heartbroken or unappreciated.
5. When you read or hear about happy couples, it makes you feel slightly sick. You feel a horrible mixture of envy and longing and as if that sort of love is a million miles away for you.
6. You torment yourself by remaining FB "friends" with an ex who has moved on and avidly monitor his newsfeed, trying to discern what every syllable means.

7. You think about your singleness a lot, and worry that you'll never meet anyone. Your anxiety over your single status is starting to affect the rest of your life and your general happiness.
8. You believe that love, for whatever reason, doesn't work out for you and wonder underneath it all (not that you'd ever admit this to anyone else) if perhaps you're destined to be alone.
9. You focus on any tiny imperfection you might have, physical or otherwise, and think it makes you ineligible for true love. You put up with sub-standard relationships because you don't think you deserve better.
10. You say to yourself or other people that all men are _____ (insert negative label), while simultaneously wanting Prince Charming to come along and transform your life.

See what I mean? Surprise!

Wanting love while thinking and behaving in this way is equivalent to eating fried food 24/7 to prepare for a summer at the beach. It's backwards. It's upside down, it's inside out. And it makes no sense. Sure, the romantic hiccups of others or the perceived faults of the opposite sex can make you feel better initially when your love life is tanking or completely non-existent. But concentrating on this sort of thing is self-sabotage. You're literally sculpting your brain for dissatisfying relationships, and nobody wants that.

So how do you get those positive love neurons humming and find a relationship that makes you smile instead of frown and skip instead of slouch? It's time to get up close and personal with neuroscience, or more specifically neuroplasticity.

Retraining your brain for love

Neuroplasticity is brain sculpting, no surgery required. Don't worry, the only tricky thing about it is remembering how to spell it. The brilliant thing about neuroplasticity is when you change what you think about and concentrate on, your brain gets on board immediately. Stop thinking about someone who broke your heart or worrying about being alone, and the pathways in your brain that associate love with pain begin to wither. Start thinking about happiness and great relationships, and your love neurons will begin building the framework for happily ever after in the love zone of your brain.

If you want to move your mind into the love zone and keep it there, neuroplasticity is about to become your best friend. Change what you give your attention to and you change your brain. I changed my brain, and as a result transformed my life and my relationships. When you see it like this, you can understand why constantly focusing on or rehashing failed romances isn't doing you any favours. If you want your own personal happily ever after you have to start to give your attention to love being brilliant and a place to have needs met. In my experience, it can be as simple and straightforward as that.

Signing up for the team

Keen to get on board the love train? Wondering where to begin? Right here.

The great thing about doing the *Unsingle* steps is you will begin to feel better straightaway. Your mind and your brain start to calm down and so do you. The immediate benefits are a sense of relief and a feeling of (finally) being on the right track romance-wise, which is the perfect starting point from which to invite true love into your life.

You have everything you need to be happy in love. Every single thing. You just need to flip the switch and retrain your brain for love.

Ten steps to finding true love

So how did I say goodbye to singledom and attract the love I wanted into my life? I developed my own ten steps to give my neural pathways an update and retrain my brain for love. When I started this journey I had no map. I was not a relationship expert and had no qualifications in the field. But the knowledge that the mind was incredibly powerful was not new to me. Through my work I met with bestselling authors in the personal development and mind-body-spirit genre and heard – on a daily basis – that for most of our issues and questions, the answer lies within. However until I learnt about neuroplasticity and the love zone within my brain, I didn't think this applied to matters of the heart. I believe I thought the song had it right: that I couldn't hurry love, that I had to wait and that it didn't come easy. The idea that perhaps I could hurry it, I didn't have to wait forever and that it might come easier than expected gave me the impetus to read everything I could on how our brains rewire themselves and find methods and processes to help it along its way. I looked to people as varied as Einstein, Shakti Gawain and Napoleon Hill for inspiration then I cut my own path and handed the process over to love. I decided to trust in it and trust in myself and what transpired is that which you will read about here.

The steps that follow transformed me from single and sick of it to meeting the love of my life within five months and being proposed to two weeks after that. Seven years later I'm happier than I've ever been with a husband who I cherish more every day. But I know if I hadn't decided to unsingle myself we would have never made the connection. I would still be sitting alone on my couch wondering what I was doing wrong.

In case you haven't guessed *Unsingle* is all about love and bringing it to you sooner rather than later. Following my ten steps you'll learn how to utilise Einstein's favourite mind tool to bring you the relationship of your dreams, and you'll be shown how to negotiate any bumps in the road along the way. So what are we waiting for? Here is a quick overview of the steps to get you started.

'Part 1: Moving your mind into the love zone' covers the first three steps. 'Step 1: Clearing the way' gets you to look at your environment in a new way. It explains how your environment affects you and how surrounding yourself with the wrong things can actually block love from coming to you. You are introduced to mental functioning and discover how your neural pathways are forged and maintained by what you think about, look at, focus on and believe in. Here you'll get the opportunity to modify your living space to support your new journey. 'Step 2: Finding treasure' is all about focus. It's about making something that visually represents true love to you and putting your true love story on the map. You'll be creating a treasure map or treasure app in your choice of media filled with pictures, personal photos, words and phrases that evoke happily ever after to you. Creating it will help you begin to forge new neural pathways that support positive beliefs about love. Finally, in 'Step 3: Flipping the switch' – it's time to establish a daily routine and flip the switch on any negative thoughts about your singleness, using the power of your mind to your own advantage. You'll hear stories about people as diverse as Albert Einstein and Sara Blakely (the world's first female self-made billionaire) using their imagination to achieve their goals. You'll learn how to use this innate ability to help you achieve your goal – a love that lasts forever.

Next comes 'Part 2: Keeping your mind in the love zone' which will guide you through the next four steps. 'Step 4: Bumps in the road' provides you with a useful tool to get you through any difficult situations you may encounter on the way to unsingling yourself. It helps you avoid slipping back into your old way of thinking and undoing all the good work that your focus and attention on love has done, using the technique developed in the previous step and integrating it into your everyday life. The next step, 'Step 5: Negativity diet', is about reducing the volume of negative love input in your life and amping up the positive.

Following this comes 'Step 6: Minding the gap', where you'll learn about the yay! experiment, the singing grocer and why it's important to 'mind the gap'. We'll talk about clever ways to keep yourself feeling positive while you're waiting for true love to arrive in your life. 'Step 7: False starts' focuses on how to approach this final stage of unsingling. Because you've been doing such great work focusing on love, your increased happiness and confidence will often result in receiving extra attention from the opposite sex, so here you'll receive advice about negotiating the intricacies of dating along with help in recognising the difference between true love and false starts. You'll hear the story of 'The Wrong Man' and be introduced to the concepts of the thunderbolt and the slow burner.

Finally comes 'Part 3: Your true love relationship' covering the last three steps. 'Step 8: True love' kicks in once you've found your person and are no longer in the waiting room of love – yay! Congratulations. This step clears up a few common myths about true love and gives suggestions and advice on how to maintain the great relationship you've found. Once you're at 'Step 9: Socialising unsingle style' it's party time! Now that you have someone to share your life with, social events that include a 'plus one' are going to be a lot more fun. This chapter also offers helpful hints on how to integrate your unsingled status into the rest of your life, discussing the importance of discretion and how to approach time spent with friends who don't share your positive beliefs about love. In the final chapter, 'Step 10: Home is where the heart is', you've come full circle. You modified your living environment with great success at the start of your unsingling journey, so it's appropriate that we end our time together here. Sooner or later, moving in together will be part of your true love experience and your home is where the two of you rest and spend precious time together. You'll learn easy ways to create and maintain a harmonious living space that supports you as a couple.

So if it's time for you to start your unsingling, read on. Your love zone is waiting. Retraining your brain for love starts now!

Part 1

Moving your mind into the love zone

Step 1
Clearing the way

Nothing is either good or bad, but thinking makes it so.
— William Shakespeare

Here you are at the start of your unsingling journey. You're ready to meet the love of your life and leave your single status behind. Ready to move forward, shift your relationship gear out of neutral and let love have its way with you. And you're ready to acknowledge that this is going to be an inside job. Because no matter what you've been saying to yourself – that you have no blocks to love, that you've been ready for years – if you've wanted a relationship for a significant amount of time and it hasn't materialised, something has been standing in your way. It has nothing to do with how you look, the way you dress, where you live or what you do. It is, I believe, wholly attributable to what is going on inside your mind, to your perceptions and beliefs when it comes to love.

It's those perceptions and beliefs that need an adjustment, because when you replace the idea that true love is a random event assigned to other lucky people with the knowledge that true love is anything but random and meant for you too, you'll dissolve the barrier which has been standing in your way. *Unsingle* is designed specifically to reignite your belief in love that lasts, to help you not only believe in that sort of love again but to feel it right next to you. So close you know it's meant for you. When you make that internal change and shift in your attitudes and emotions, it won't be long before everything around you changes. And you'll meet that one special person you get to live with and love for the rest of your life.

This first step, 'Clearing the way', is not about being a domestic goddess. It's about clearing the way for love. Your home could be gleaming, immaculate and pristine and still be full of things that are keeping happily ever after from your door. Remember the ten signs that you aren't playing for Team Love? The list of defensive thoughts and beliefs you developed to protect your heart that kept love at arm's length without your knowledge? If you take the time to look around you, you might find those negative attitudes and ideas have found a way into your living space without you even realising it. You could be surrounded by items that you look at every day without realising they're working against you and your deepest desires. I'm going to repeat that because it's important: there could be things in your everyday life that are working against you, barring you from unsingling yourself. They could be habits you've developed or items you don't even consciously think about, as they're literally and figuratively part of the furniture. Once you begin looking at your environment through your unsingle filter you might be quite surprised by what you find.

Getting choosy

So let's get started. Look at the things that surround you from the perspective of someone who's ready for love. First, glance at the books you have on your bookshelf or perched on your bedside table. If any of them have titles along the lines of *Single is Fab, All Men Are* _____ or *10 Reasons Love Never Works Out*, stop for a moment and ask yourself what message those titles are sending out. If a friend was visiting your place for the first time and saw those books on your shelves, would they get the impression true love was just around the corner for you? Probably not. Those phrases and words are subliminally going into your psyche every time you glance at them. And even though some might like to argue they have no impact on you, they do (I'll explain how shortly). This is not an indictment on the quality of these books. The books in and of themselves may be excellent – for someone who has no interest in finding true love. But for the purpose of unsingling they need to be either thrown away or stored out of your line of sight for the duration of the unsingling process.

The same rule applies to magazines you have lying around with headlines screaming 'Heading for the divorce courts', 'It's over' or 'The love rat strikes again'. However oblivious or immune you might believe yourself to be to this sort of influence, or however far removed you think you are from the celebrities' lives they're referring to, I'd like you to humour me and put them out of sight for the time being. Add them to your box of books if you like. Or if you threw away your books, feel free to do the same here.

As you go through each step you'll notice an increase in your awareness. You will become aware of how many choices you make *every day* about what you give your attention to. Attention is a powerful thing and these steps have been deliberately designed for you to start noticing where you direct your attention. And by being conscious of this you're going to start making better, more informed choices. You're going to redirect that attention and ask yourself questions rather than acting automatically, out of habit.

It's okay to start making different choices, because when you make the conscious decision to shift your focus to seek out what is right with love – switching your homing beacon away from what is wrong – things in your life will begin to shift. Those lurid headlines will lose their appeal. And you will be pleasantly surprised by how many examples of true love appear right in front of you. So unless the magazines you usually buy are positive or completely neutral when it comes to relationships, leave them out of your shopping trolley. Buy a magazine that focuses on fashion or travel or interior design. Those negative love messages are no longer for you.

Accentuating the positive

Anyone concerned that this strategy of removing negative love messages is overzealous, convinced that words and phrases don't have that much influence or power, might want to read Dr Masuro Emoto's *New York Times* bestseller, *The Hidden Messages in Water*. To demonstrate the effect words have – and remembering water comprises around 80 per cent of our bodies – he photographed molecules of distilled water through a dark field microscope. Their shape was a regular, unremarkable hexagon. He took that same water and put it in two separate containers, and taped the words 'Chi of love' on one bottle and 'You make me sick, I'm going to kill you' on another and left them overnight.

The next morning Dr Emoto took photos through the same dark field microscope of the molecules of the water from each container. The molecules that had been exposed to the words of love had transformed into delicate, refined crystalline shapes, so exquisitely beautiful you might never want to stop gazing at them. In contrast, the molecules exposed to the harsh words were distorted, irregular and, spookily enough, contained an outline of what looked like a small figure holding a gun. Dr Emoto got similar results when he exposed the water to positive and negative pictures and images.

As our bodies are mostly water, it follows that words or phrases we're exposed to on a regular basis affect us too. In fact there's significant scientific evidence supporting the premise that words and images affect us on a cellular level. So why not give your psyche a rest and surround yourself with words and images of love, particularly while you're in the process of unsingling yourself?

A picture tells a thousand words

With this research in mind, what about the pictures you have hanging on the walls of your home? They might be posters, paintings, photos, postcards. What do they depict? Looking with an objective eye can be quite illuminating, because what's happening on the inside often finds a way to express itself on the outside. And art is a way we express ourselves. So take a second look at that lonely windswept landscape, the print of the heart split down the middle or the solitary, unsmiling person staring out at you. Really look at them. No matter how artistic or extraordinary they are, if there is a negative association with any of them, triggering feelings of loneliness, numbness or heartbreak, you need to take them down and sell, donate or store them. If they're valuable and you're very attached to them, store them well. Don't try to defend any items or negotiate with yourself that you'll just keep this one up because your mother or sister gave it to you, you spent a lot of money on it, it goes with your colour scheme and so on. No-one can tell you how to feel about anything; you are the only one who knows how something affects you, who knows if looking at it makes you feel bad about your romantic prospects or about life in general. And if it does, for any reason, it needs to be taken down.

Speaking of the importance of the way you feel about something and how personal those feelings are, let's say you have a photographic print of a beach at sunset. This picture could have a number of different personal meanings depending on the circumstances that brought it into your home. Perhaps you bought it because you loved the drama of the sun's rays pouring from behind the clouds. Or maybe it was a gift from a friend or family member and you couldn't believe how perfectly they'd chosen for you. You love gazing at it and having it there makes you feel optimistic and cheerful, or just plain good. Fantastic, leave it up, enjoy it. But if the exact same print had been bought after spending a holiday at that particular beach with your ex and you kept it when you divided your things because at the time you wanted it, you might have very different feelings about it now. Shakespeare was onto something when he said that nothing is either good or bad but thinking makes it so. The picture is fine. There is absolutely nothing wrong with the picture. It is how the picture makes you feel and the thoughts it evokes. That's what's important. Because if it makes your heart sink even a little every time you look at it, or you can never glance at it without being reminded of the love that ended, it's not working for you is it?

It doesn't take long to segue from a brief recollection of a relationship that ended badly to the familiar avalanche of pain linked to the heartbreak that followed. Unsingling is about letting that go in a big way. It's about getting excited, happy and anticipatory. It's about not going for the ride down Pain Highway. Those neural memory pathways need to be zapped. You want them gone. Make sure what you have on your walls supports your goal to reignite your belief in happily ever after. If it doesn't, remove it straightaway. And if you have nowhere to store your items, then for the moment prop them up facing the wall until you can get some paper to wrap them in. Just so long as you're no longer looking at them, you're doing well.

You can change your mind

Neuroplasticity is the name for the scientific discovery that has proven via neural imaging that the brain is constantly rewiring itself based on our daily experiences, that what we give our attention to shapes our brain, our mind and our relationships. It refers to the ability of the human brain to change its neural connectivity as a result of one's experiences and tells us that neural pathways are forged and maintained by what we think about, look at, focus on and believe in today. Therefore it is possible to change our habitual thoughts and forge new neural pathways by directing ourselves to concentrate on what we want to see and experience.

What this science means to us is that, by changing what we focus on and give our attention to we are able to disengage old neural pathways that associate love with pain, and replace them with pathways that associate love with happiness. Yay! Focused attention stimulates neural firing, which creates new neural pathways. You can literally 'change your mind' when it comes to how you perceive and experience love and relationships. All good news when you're in the process of unsingling yourself.

Expecting someone?

Let's move to the most personal room of all. What does your bedroom look like? Asking whether a room's contents are conducive to inviting love in or are pushing love out is particularly valid when it comes to your bedroom. Now that you have an understanding of what your living environment has been saying, you might glance around your bedroom and realise some minor or major adjustments need to be made.

Perhaps there is literally no room for anyone else to come into your life – is the side of the bed you don't sleep on covered with magazines, your iPad, books, work reports or discarded clothes? Maybe it's your subconscious trying to make up for the fact there is no-one sleeping peacefully on the other side, or perhaps you're trying to create a protective wall. Or maybe you're just a bit messy. It doesn't really matter. The message it is sending out is clear: you may as well have a sign flashing above your bed saying 'I'm not expecting anyone to sleep with me here – ever!' Not a message you want to be sending out while in the process of unsingling yourself. Both sides need to be kept clear and inviting, underlining the fact that you are ready for love, for someone to share your life.

If you're thinking this is ridiculous because of course you'd clean up your bed if a new fellow had come into your life, you're somewhat missing the point. What do people say when they're in a café waiting for someone to join them and you ask if you can have the unused seat at their table? They smile and say, 'Sorry, I'm expecting someone'. And you respect that. You don't put your shopping on the chair anyway. Because although there's no-one sitting there right now, you know they're on their way. The person sitting there has told you. They're coming. There is an energy around expectancy that draws things to you. And Step 1 is about using that energy to your advantage.

Bed is an important part of life and of unsingleness. It's where you relax, sleep, snuggle, make love. And that space is for your mate. You are making room for what you want in your life. There's nothing half-hearted in the decision to unsingle yourself; it's not a case of 'Well, yeah maybe I'd like to have someone someday'. It's about making up your mind regarding what you will have in your life, sooner rather than later. It's about psychology and the power of expectancy. Expectation is a powerful force. It's stronger than hope. Clearing that space is putting a distinct message out into the universe that you are expecting someone, just as clearly as a pile of stuff obscuring half of your bed is saying you're not. Imagine you're a sports pro playing for Team Love and your environment is your cheer squad. You want your squad to be sending out a very clear and unequivocal message: 'What do we want? Love! When do we want it? Now!' If it wouldn't pass the cheer test, clean it up.

Wardrobe malfunction

Let's administer the same treatment to your wardrobe. Open its doors and have a look. There may not be anything immediately obvious but don't close it up just yet. Think about whether you have any clothing or bags that have phrases written across them, and ensure those words are in line with what you want. This includes any items like sassy T-shirts that say 'Single and fabulous'. Yes, you are currently single and fabulous but you want to be unsingle and fabulous so you know what to do. Ditto any clothing or bags that have messages like 'Love ends and hearts break' emblazoned across them. No matter how cool the label, they need to go because neither statement is where you want to be.

You also need to consider pieces that hold sad or bad memories, like that gorgeous dress given to you by an ex or perhaps that you bought for a special event that turned into a nightmare because the two of you broke up. That dress is never going to make you feel good about love and relationships. The truth is, no matter how pretty or expensive, the dress is carrying that negative energy forward. Whenever you look at it, touch it or wear it – unless you're lucky enough to have developed incident-specific amnesia about that night – you'll remember the hurt. As already mentioned, unsingling is about not going for that ride. It's about turning your head to face your present and your future. And that means removing from your space anything that is keeping those negative neural pathways pulsing. So in the spirit of unsingling yourself, even if you look great when you wear it, if it makes you feel not-so-good it has to go. Sell it on eBay if you like and buy something new with the proceeds. The same goes for any items you may have liberated from any previous partners, like the super-soft T-shirt you sleep in (not to be sold on eBay, obviously). It doesn't matter if it is the most comfortable nightwear in existence. It's over. You've moved on. Throw. It. In. The. Bin.

Use this process throughout your entire home or living space, and now you know what you are looking for it shouldn't take too long. The blender you inherited when you divided your things needs to go. So too the toothbrush left behind. And if you have a garage or carport that has two spaces, then – just like keeping both sides of your bed clear and inviting – you need to make sure you park neatly in one space, leaving room for another car. Again, this is about expectation and crystal clear intentions.

If you're in a share house you don't have complete control over every item but you can still keep your energy away from anything that makes you feel uneasy about love. Don't pick up the magazine touting the latest marriage scandal or look at the sad-sack, lonely print your flatmate has mounted in pride of place. Don't give them any attention at all. It may take a little restraint not to reach for the shiny new weekly your housemate bought. But similar to avoiding the quick fix of a sweet treat because you don't want to spoil the delicious meal you have planned, your effort will be worth it. If, however, you absolutely can't resist picking it up, turn straight to the pages on what people were wearing and ignore the cover story completely. Don't tell yourself you'll read a few sentences just to find out what happened and then you'll forget about it; the mind doesn't work like that. You give it something juicy to latch onto and it will latch on every time.

Think clear, clean canvas because that's what Step 1 is all about. The next few chapters are about filling your mind with wonderful thoughts and images of true love, happiness, joy and romance. In fact, you're going to saturate yourself in it, so much so your brain will be too preoccupied with the good stuff to have any interest in anything else. You're going to stop focusing on the relationship troubles of the rich and famous – or anyone else for that matter – and leave them to their business. Instead you're going to think about yourself and what you want, flipping the switch on all your reasons for staying single and turning them on their head, effectively losing your fear of the love and intimacy you've been craving. All aboard!

Clearing the way checklist

💙 Unsingling is about making a decision and sticking to it. It's not about maybe, sorta, kinda wanting true love. It is about deciding what you will have and expecting it, harnessing the power of your mind and directing it to focus on love.

💙 Unsingling is about replacing your belief that true love is a faraway place meant for other people with the understanding that true love is meant for you too. It is designed to help you change your beliefs about love, to demystify and make accessible the prospect of sharing your life with someone who truly loves you.

💙 Expectancy is a powerful force. Use it to your advantage. Set up your home, particularly your bedroom, as if you already have the relationship you desire.

💙 Neuroplasticity is the scientific discovery that has proven via neural imaging that the brain is constantly rewiring itself based on daily experiences and where attention is focused. In unsingling terms, this means you can 'change your mind' when it comes to how you perceive and experience love relationships.

💙 Words and phrases are powerful. Any books, magazines, artwork or clothing that contain negative messages about love and relationships or relish your single state need to be disposed of or put out of sight for the duration of the unsingling process.

♥ What you are feeling on the inside is often reflected in your environment, so be rigorous when you go through your living space and ensure no item is working against your belief in true love. The way you *feel* when you look at, read or hold an item will often tell you if it's working for you. Or not.

♥ Items that remind you of a relationship that ended badly should wherever.possible be disposed of. If they promote particularly strong feelings, consider throwing them away instead of donating or selling them. (Throwing items like this in the garbage can make you feel really good!)

♥ Unsingling is about getting excited, happy and anticipatory. It's about not going for the ride down Pain Highway. When you remove your attention from your previous romantic troubles or the relationship problems of others, and start to focus on love, you begin to invite it into your life. Your mind needs to be clear and ready for the steps that follow.

Step 2
Finding treasure

We are all born for love.
— Benjamin Disraeli

The first chapter was about clearing the path to love, getting any hidden landmines or silent saboteurs out of the way so you can feel supported by your environment while you unsingle yourself. You were introduced to your unsingle filter and used it to ensure there was nothing in your home that was blocking love from coming to you. You got the opportunity to nix any negative love messages and in doing so you took the first step to moving your mind into the love zone. An excellent start. In this chapter you will be using that filter again. This time, however, you'll be using it to discover things you love; images and phrases that make your heart beat a little faster and cause a nice, warm, fuzzy sensation in your chest. It's time to shake things up a bit, to stop thinking so much and start to *feel* your way. It's time to get creative.

Your treasure map

You have probably heard of inspiration boards, vision boards and dream boards. The titles vary but the concept is the same: a person has a goal and creating their board helps focus their energy toward that goal. Designers, stylists, architects, entrepreneurs, office workers, school children and countless others look to them for inspiration and use them to define and help create in their lives whatever they desire. A while ago, they were called treasure maps and for unsingling purposes we're going to use that name because it's prettier. Treasure maps also include something their derivatives don't always mention, something important which we will get to in a moment. Firstly, let's clarify exactly what we're talking about.

Treasure maps visually represent, in words, phrases and pictures, what you would like your relationship to embody. They help you form a clear image of your true love relationship. Every time you look at it you're giving your focused attention to what you want. Your neural pathways associated with love will immediately begin to respond.

Treasure maps help you start to become more selective about what you give your attention to. They help you 'get your eye in', training you to seek out examples of what true love looks like, and making filtering input second nature. This skill will be of great benefit to you as you are in the process of unsingling yourself – when you're looking for what you want you won't be giving your attention to things you don't want, and then you'll really be cooking with gas. Originally, treasure maps were made by a person gathering pictures, personal photos, images, words and phrases that were meaningful to them regarding their goal, then using these to create a collage. The collage was pieced together on a pin board or on thick card. When it was complete it was placed in a prominent place on the wall so they could gaze at it frequently. The original treasure maps always featured a happy photo of their creator in the centre of the collage. This is vital and non-negotiable content. You need to be front and centre, surrounded by images that make your heart happy.

Now there are applications (apps) available that do a lot of the work for you and your creation is saved within your PC, tablet or mobile phone. A lot of people, most notably designers and stylists, continue to use the original collage method and their boards are works of art in themselves. But there's been a consistent trend in people starting to use apps. It really comes down to personal choice and how you like to do things.

There's another benefit of treasure maps that is just as important for unsingling purposes as those we've just covered: having your own personal treasure map will help you begin to approach visual and written stimuli from a different angle, more specifically to ignore the negative and the sensational, and zero in on the good. Neural pathways associating love with happiness will begin to form and strengthen. Because when you're looking for pictures and words that invoke happiness, comfort and joy within a relationship you're going to notice how many examples of true love exist all around you. Your mind will start moving in another direction and your internal compass will begin to point due love. When you're flicking through magazines and other print media or searching the internet, you've set your homing beacon to love. It gives your psyche a rest and lets you enjoy the happy and the light, bypassing everything that is not.

Before we begin looking at the relative benefits of each method and which one would suit you best, there are a few points you might like to keep in mind. This is your first unsingling creation and you want it to reflect *you*.

Your love zone

Unsingling is a time when you get to focus on you, acknowledging your inner genius when it comes to you and your heart. So it's essential you leave everyone else's wants, wishes and desires for you out of the equation when creating your treasure map, unless they match perfectly with yours. Friends and family sometimes mistake their needs and preferences for your own, and although they're usually coming from a good and loving place they don't always know what's best for you. You have exclusive rights to that privilege. This exercise is designed to help you gain clarity about what you want. It's really not about anyone else. So unless someone has given you advice that struck a chord within you and you felt that resounding internal 'yes!' it's best practice to leave it out.

Focus on the way you want to feel

People can mess up their chance for true love by having very stringent requirements for a partner that have nothing to do with a person's character or their heart. Sometimes they search so hard in one direction, determined that their partner look a certain way, have a particular job or enjoy a certain hobby, they completely miss the most important qualities of all – qualities inherent to true love. If this has been you, it's time to shift your focus. Concentrate on how you want to *feel* and you don't have to control every aspect. Just focus on wanting to be really, really happy and you will draw to you someone who brings out that emotion in you.

It's natural to have preferences but they need to be anchored in how you want to feel when you're with the person and the sort of things you'd like to do together, not based on material or superficial concerns. Jobs, looks, hobbies are additional extras.

A person's character is the engine that drives a relationship. A man who looks after you and loves you when you are down, and who celebrates you when you've achieved something is what unsingling is about. If he happens to be a lawyer who jogs and looks like Ryan Reynolds and that's what you want, that's great. But those preferences need to be secondary to loving and being loved in the way you've always wanted, if you want to stay true to the unsingling ethos.

Those of you who don't like to relinquish control might argue, 'But I don't want to end up with someone who's …!' Would being with someone you found '…!' make you feel happy? No, it wouldn't. The feeling-good factor covers all bases. Similarly, for those who have a pastime that's extremely important to you and desperately want your partner to share your passion you need to be prepared to be flexible. Your true love may be passionate about you, and though he supports your hobby it's not his. This doesn't mean shared interests are a no-no. But just because you love running and he does marathons doesn't mean you are an emotional match. You very well might be, but don't prioritise 'has to love running' above 'has to be a good man and take care of my heart'.

The perfect man for you may have given up running when he started to wear long pants but he makes you feel so good, so loved, safe and secure you find you don't care. Outsource the details to love and it will surpass every expectation you've ever had. For any and every argument you can come up with on this point, love is the answer. It just is. It's all you ever need to know. When you make feeling loved in your relationship your top priority, everything else falls into place.

True love

The objective of unsingling is true love. We've talked a little about what it isn't in the previous points, so let's define what it is, seeing it's the reason we're all here. True love can come to you in as many different packages, sizes and colours as there are people in the universe. It doesn't discriminate and it doesn't care whether you're black or white, straight or gay, married or committed without the ring. It's about two hearts in sync with each other. Whatever it looks like, it always *feels* the same. It makes you feel as though you are enough just as you are. It makes you feel safe and cared for. It makes you feel seen. Understood. And although it isn't perfect, it is equal. Every bit of love, caring, concern and encouragement you put into your relationship comes right back to you. It might come back in a different way, but it balances out. And you know in your heart you've met your person, the one who is right for you. Your true love.

Our inherent longing for this sort of love is what drives us, I believe. The knowing inside us that to love and be loved, to have fun and laugh is what we're here for. True love is amazing and although it feels pretty miraculous, you're not asking to walk on water. It's what you were designed for. Unsingling is about demystifying true love by acknowledging its normalcy, taking it from the realms of Never Never Land and placing it squarely in your own backyard.

Now that you know a little more on what a treasure map is and is not about, it's time for you to evaluate and decide which of the two methods you'd prefer to use – a treasure app or a handmade treasure map. Either way you'll have your own little work of art.

A *treasure app*

This first method is the latest one. Treasure apps are specifically tailored for your iPad, tablet, PC or phone. If you like small, portable, compact and concise, and are reasonably technologically adept, the app method is probably the one for you. No muss, no fuss. For people who have limited time, this approach is quick and easy.

If you know what you want and have a pretty clear picture in your mind of what your true love relationship looks like, this version is for you. Perhaps you know you want to get married, you'd like to have a family and a home, dream of honeymooning in the Maldives and so on. Or alternatively you know you don't want the ring; you want a partner but no children; you'd like to holiday in France and your dream is to live near the water.

For either, writing a list of image searches should be easy.

First example: you want to get married and honeymoon somewhere with crystal clear water. You'd like to have a family and a home. Your image search list might include: St Martin's Church, bride and groom, oceanfront villa on tropical island, couple hugging, beautiful home, young family.

Second example: you don't mind whether you get married or not; you want a partner but no children; you'd like to holiday in France and your dream is to live near the water; you like skiing. Your image search list might include: wine tasting, couple laughing, the Eiffel Tower, couple skiing, apartment with balcony and view of ocean.

Doing a search on Google Images will net you a wide selection of general pictures. Often there's also an app feature for you to write your own text, which is important because you'll want words and phrases included. I've gone into more detail on the kinds of suitable phrases in the second method. For now things like 'love', 'true love', 'yes!', 'blissfully happy' and 'couldn't be better!' scattered throughout are perfect to create the effect you're going for.

Putting yourself in the picture

You may also have some personal photos you would like to include. There needs to be *at least one photo of you* where you are smiling or laughing placed in the centre of your masterpiece. The app's whole purpose is so you see yourself already immersed in the life you want. And the original handmade versions always have a central photo of the map's creator surrounded by that which they desire, without which it really could apply to anyone.

Prices for vision-board type apps range from around AU$1 up to about $13. Generally, the more the app costs the more features and versatility it has. Obviously, you need to check them all out and see which suits your needs best. HappyTapper Vision Board on iTunes and Vision Board PRO by Astraport on Google Play are a couple of examples that rate well. Notesplus, also on iTunes, isn't specifically designed to create treasure maps but it has great features that make creating a board very easy and it's a lot more flexible than most of the others. Many of the apps will allow you a trial run so you can see for yourself how they operate and how user friendly they are.

Space is limited with a treasure app, and if you're putting it onto your mobile phone, even more so. If, when you read on, you realise you want a more expansive version and have a large number of images and phrases you want to incorporate, a handmade treasure map might be better for you. If you're satisfied with a few images and your own photo, you'll have your treasure app with you wherever you go and can look at it often during the day. Or perhaps you might decide to create both versions and have the best of both worlds. It's completely up to you.

Moving pictures

The other feature of most treasure apps – the slideshow – is designed for you to make your own little feature with personal pictures of you smiling, interspersed with pictures and phrases that represent love and happiness to you. Watching it on your way to work while sitting on the train or bus will help move your mind into the love zone. And when you get home you can prop your iPad or device somewhere visible and have it playing on a loop, just like a digital photo frame, something inspiring that works for you in the background while you prepare a meal or listen to music. The best thing about the slideshow is that when you glance at it, it gives you a buzz without you having to lift a finger.

Handmade treasure map

If you prefer, you can make your treasure map the old-fashioned way. It's definitely the more retro and hands-on approach because you need to gather magazines or print from the internet to find your treasure, pictures that speak to you of true love.

So if this method is for you, collect your magazines, or if you don't really buy them ask friends and family if you can have their discards. The Sunday supplements from the newspaper are good and even your local newspaper might have usable content. Also keep an eye out for free publications, brochures and the like when you're shopping. The magazines in stands outside real estate agents, travel agents and health food stores can be great. Thrift stores and op shops also sell magazines really cheaply. It doesn't matter if they're a few years old because when it comes to love, the content will be about the same.

You'll need a piece of thick cardboard and at least one photo of you that you love because you look so happy, plus some glue and scissors, and that's about it. This is definitely the more time-consuming method but you can make it exactly to your specifications. You're not limited space-wise. And like the inspiration boards designers and stylists create, it can be your own little work of art. So take your time if you feel so inclined because you're going to be looking at it a lot. And it's going to make you feel really, really good.

What does love look like to you?

When you start to look through your magazines or scan the internet, if you notice a flash of interest or a rush of warmth when looking at a particular picture, cut it out or print it and put it aside – even if it's something you weren't previously aware you wanted. This exercise is about letting your feelings do the talking. You might find the simple things hold the greatest appeal. It might be a couple snuggling on a couch looking blissful and you realise this everyday occurrence would make you supremely happy. Even if you think it's a bit pedestrian, that doesn't matter. If it speaks to you it's worth including. Or you might see a picture of something extraordinary: people amidst a riot of colour at a festival in India and think how amazing that

would be to do with your love. Even if you've never travelled before or never contemplated going to India, add it to your pile. You're letting your feelings do the talking so allow them to guide you.

Maybe your dream is to start a family. Find a picture of a young family doing something fun. Or if you already have children, find a picture of something you would all enjoy, perhaps a trip to Disneyland or Dreamworld. Cut away. If you've always wanted to honeymoon in Fiji, or there's a particular church or historic building you've dreamt about getting married in, go and take a photo of it or download a picture of it from the internet and print. Make your treasure map as personally meaningful to you as you can. But only do this if it's fun. There should be nothing stressful about this process at all. If time is an issue and the pictures from the magazines are good enough and make you feel good, stick with them. Whatever makes you feel anticipatory and optimistic about falling in love, add it to your pile.

If your parents or grandparents have one of those great love stories and you aspire to have the same, paste a photo of them in there, preferably one in which they both look happy and loved up. Remember what I talked about in the first chapter – it's all about how a picture makes you feel. That applies twice here. Including a photo of a couple you see as a success helps you focus on success in love. If you don't know anyone whose relationship you'd like to emulate, you can turn to celebrities or public figures for inspiration. Best not to include the ones that are on the cover of the tabloids every week, but if you notice couples with a public profile who, when you look at their picture, you feel the love, include them. Perhaps they represent something special to you, or you know they're back-story and always thought it sounded romantic and real. If that's the case, cut out their picture and include it in your map.

Word perfect

The right words and phrases on your map can also really give you a lift, so make sure you include them. Phrases like 'meet the new love of my life' are what you're looking for. It doesn't matter if it's the ad line for a new washing machine, just cut out the sentence. Similarly anything like 'the perfect marriage' would be a great affirmation to have up there if you want to get married. It doesn't matter if it's the title of an article about a recently appointed CEO, all you'll be using is the headline. You can also use words taken from advertising lines such as 'love Magnum' can provide you with the word 'love', for example.

What you definitely *do not* want to include are phrases like 'working on it', 'problem solving', even 'making up is fun to do'. Anything that refers to struggle, work, effort, arguments, difficulties is to be given an extremely wide berth. Ensure all words and phrases articulate what you want in your life, in an upbeat way. This is your creation so be very selective about what you include. You don't want to focus on and potentially invite anything problematical or hard, do you? So don't include it.

Already there

If you want to take your treasure map to a whole new level, superimpose a picture of yourself into a scene that you wish to experience. You should till have your own photo front and centre, but this approach also has you participating *within* the scene of one or more of the surrounding pictures.

Say you see a photo in a magazine of a wine tasting at a beautiful rustic winery and you think that's something you'd really enjoy doing with your love. There are people in the background of the shot, slightly blurred for artistic effect and an empty expanse in the foreground. You might have a photo of yourself where you are smiling and happy and know would blend in well. If you carefully cut out your image from your photo then glue it in the foreground, doing your best to ensure its placement is realistic regarding perspective, from a slight distance it will look as if you are really there. If you like, you can also use a marker to draw an arrow to one of the blurred men standing in the background and write 'my true love'. If there's no-one suitable in the shot you can imagine he was the one taking the photo. The point is to see yourself already immersed in the life you desire.

Colour printing from the internet can be helpful with this, as you can be more specific about the location if there's some place in particular you want represented on your map. If you don't have the time or inclination to go this far, that's fine; a happy photo of you in the middle of your board surrounded by images and words that relate to your deepest desires will work beautifully, so don't worry. But for those of you to whom the idea appeals, these types of images place you there as a participant, already exactly where you want to be.

Your happy place

When you have the pictures, words and phrases you wish to include, lay out your piece of cardboard and play around with different placements until looking at it puts a smile on your face. It doesn't have to be perfect – as long as looking at it takes you to your happy place you've done well. Once it's complete put it up opposite your bed using an adhesive that won't mark your walls. Then stand back and admire your handiwork. It will be the first thing you see in the morning and the last thing you see at night, and that's when you'll be focusing on it the most. If you've done your map using an app, you'll also be looking at it during these times, probably with your tablet or phone sitting on your lap or propped up in front of you.

We'll talk about implementing a daily routine in the next chapter, but for now just enjoy it. You have a way to go yet, but things are starting to move in the right direction. Shifts are happening and you're on your way. Can you feel it?

Feng shui for love

Right at the start of my unsingling journey I had a very interesting experience. Home alone after work one evening I wasn't even conscious of how jangled I was until the electricity went out. Luckily I found some candles and lit them. Then instead of picking up a book or magazine as I usually would have done I simply sat, watching the flickering light on the walls. After a few minutes of just breathing and watching, my impatience faded and the most amazing calm came over me. I couldn't remember ever feeling so calm. When the lights came back on I was disappointed. The magic was over.

But that brief interlude reminded me of something I'd forgotten as my unhappiness over being single grew: the importance of peace and feeling connected to myself and my home. I somehow knew that part of the path to meeting someone I could relax with was to relax more in the here and now. That meant making my house feel softer, more inviting and taking the time occasionally to simply 'be'. So I invested in some nicer candles, bought fresh flowers and arranged them in vases, and consulted my favourite *feng shui* books to give me some ideas.

Firstly I looked up where the 'love and relationships' section was in my home, which happened to be my kitchen. It didn't look very inspiring. I decided to use the leftover pictures from my original treasure map, which was already hanging in my bedroom, to make myself a second one. I placed the second map on the kitchen's far wall and put my salt lamp in front of it. I left it on constantly, as per the *feng shui* suggestion; it cast the most beautiful rosy glow over my pictures day and night. And every time I looked at it I felt assured that things were in motion even while I was asleep or out at work and too busy to be thinking about love. There was something very steady and reassuring about having it there as I ran in and out, living my life. I'd glance over and see myself amidst so much love and it made me so happy. I was comforted by its presence.

Just in case any of you're wondering where the 'love and relationships' area is in your home or living space, let me give you the world's shortest course in feng shui for love. Your home or living space is divided into nine basic sections, represented on a bagua map (see below). The front entrance is always located somewhere along the 'knowledge – career – travel' line. For example, if your front door is to the far left of the front wall of your home, it would be located in your 'knowledge' section; far right it would be in your 'travel' area. Smack bang in the middle would mean your front door is in your 'career' section. If the door through which you regularly enter and exit your home is at the back of your house, then you need to swing the bagua map to face the other way. Wherever you always enter and leave your home from is considered your 'front' entrance, even if it's in the back of your house. You need to orient your map that way.

From your 'front' entrance, whatever room or area that is in the furthest right-hand corner of your living space is your 'love and relationships' section. And if you want to jazz it up put a treasure map or treasure app here, a lamp that casts a soft glow, a print of lovers embracing, written affirmations or all of the above – they're all things a feng shui consultant would advise if you'd asked them to help you spark up your love life. They'd also suggest you place any ornaments that are in pairs here. Suggested colours to activate your 'love and relationships' area are pinks, reds and whites. Items related to love that you place here represent another level of your environment supporting you.

Bagua map

WEALTH & PROSPERITY	FAME & REPUTATION	LOVE & RELATIONSHIPS
Purples, Blues, Reds	Reds, Oranges	Pinks, Reds, White
	Fire Element	
FAMILY	HEALTH & WELLBEING	CHILDREN & CREATIVITY
Greens, Blues	Yellows, Earth tones	Whites, Pastels
Wood Element	**Earth Element**	**Metal Element**
KNOWLEDGE & SELF-CULTIVATION	CAREER	TRAVEL & HELPFUL PEOPLE
Blues, Greens	Black	Greys, Silver
	Water Element	

'Front' door alignment

Finding treasure checklist

♥ Treasure maps visually represent in words, phrases and pictures what you would like your life to embody – in this instance the relationship you desire.

♥ Your treasure map and its content are about you and your wishes. Don't feel you have to include anyone else's viewpoint unless it matches your own. You are the only one who knows what is important and appeals to you.

❤ Keep in mind the priorities of unsingling when choosing what pictures and phrases to include. Your first priority is always true love. Priorities such as wanting a lawyer who looks like Ryan Reynolds and jogs every day need to appear lower on your list of wishes compared to qualities such as kindness, intelligence, humour, openness and an ability to love you with his whole heart, if you want to stay true to the unsingling ethos.

❤ Create your treasure map in your choice of media and fill it with pictures, personal photos, words and phrases that for you evoke love and happily ever after. You'll have your little work of art up in your home, or on your phone, computer or iPad. Your treasure map or app shows explicitly the life you want to be living with your true love.

❤ If you've created a slideshow on your treasure app, having it playing nearby when you're at home can really give you a boost. If you're interested in feng shui you can have it playing in your 'love and relationships' section along with other items that represent love to you.

❤ Creating a treasure map helps you begin using your unsingle filter to notice and zero in on the examples of true love all around you and to define what it means to you. It helps you focus on what you want and filter out input you don't, a skill you will use continually throughout the unsingling process.

❤ Your treasure map always features a photo of you in the centre, looking great and genuinely happy.

♥ Include cut-outs of words and phrases that speak to you. Never include words or phrases that denote struggle, hard work, disharmony or anything you do not wish to experience in your relationship. Your treasure map is a pure pleasure zone. If you don't want it, don't include it.

♥ If you have a specific place you want represented, colour-printing images from the internet can be a great way to tailor your treasure map to your wishes. Careful placement of a cut-out photo of you as a participant within pictures of places you want to go with your love can take your map to another level.

Step 3
Flipping the switch

Imagination is more important than knowledge.
— Albert Einstein

So far you've done some clearing out and clarifying. You've cleared your living space of any blocks to love. You've also created something beautiful that has helped define exactly what it is you do want – something that, when you look at it, helps you feel the love, the excitement. This means you're in a better place to take a breath and look inside. To acknowledge where you are – which isn't quite as intimidating now that you know where you want to go!

Before we move on to creating all sorts of positive visualisations, thoughts and statements, it's important to consider what's going on inside you, whether you have any sticky little issues or blocks that can significantly reduce the effectiveness of the positive work you do and the ease with which you can do it. We've all got "stuff". Sometimes it can get in our way and hold us back from creating the life we truly want.

I want to introduce you to a fabulous technique that's been around for a while and is now gaining international recognition. It dovetails very nicely with what we've been talking about that's happening within your neural pathways, and is the single most effective way I have found to clear the way internally so that you can fast-track retraining your brain for love.

Turning it down a notch

Whether or not you've had bad experiences with regards to love, the thought of opening up can be a scary thing. Maybe you've longed for love but never really let yourself go there. Maybe you loved someone and you got hurt. Or maybe you simply feel worn down, not by terrible experiences but by never getting what you needed from your partner or from a series of relationships that didn't work out. Disappointments and difficult times can embed themselves in the love zone of your brain, making you quick to react to even a hint of possible pain.

Our brains are wired for safety. Evolution designed us to make sure we put on our running skins and got going if something ferocious and fangy was chasing us. And it worked. We're still here, so we made it. Well done us. But that threat response – which we know as the 'fight or flight' response – has transmuted into something different these days. Most of our modern perceived 'threats' are no longer from a fear of being eaten alive. They come from a number of sources, such as work-related stress or financial troubles – and, for some, from fear of emotional pain. And they're rooted in previous experiences that have become hardwired into our brains, leading to an expectation of similar painful experiences in the present and future. Time to turn this response down a notch. Love shines best in a peaceful heart.

If it's there, it's there

Shifting negative beliefs, moving ahead and inviting in a significantly happier future, romance-wise, is why you're here. But at times at the beginning of your unsingling journey you might find yourself in something of an emotional cul-de-sac. You've increased your awareness, determined to move your mind to a place that works for you but along with this increased awareness you realise the tape playing in your head – the background mental chatter when it comes to love – isn't always good.

This is normal and rather than beating yourself up for not being perfect, you should give yourself a pat on the back for recognising those old tracks playing in your thoughts. Our positive, positive, positive culture can make you feel as if you have to push down what you're really thinking and feeling and that doesn't work either. If you feel something is blocking you from moving ahead you need a tool to get to it and move through it. Don't get me wrong, I get positive. I really do. I ran a bookshop where positive thinking was practically part of the job description. But if a feeling is there, it's there. Pretending it isn't won't make it go away and stuffing it down only keeps it right there with you.

Facing your negative feelings around love might sound counterintuitive to the whole unsingle ethos, yet it's not. I'm not suggesting, nor will I ever suggest, you zero in and focus on the pain associated with past relationships. We're taking things step by step to see that you don't. But you don't need to be piling self-judgement on top of fear. It just makes you more scared and freezes you in place.

If there's a nagging voice that won't quit, you need to work with it for a while, accept it, accept yourself and retrain your brain to let it go. And once you've let 'it' go, whatever 'it' is for you, the blocks will come down, your love quotient will go up and you can move ahead. You don't buy a nice new cookbook and beautiful ingredients to prepare your first dish in a dirty kitchen. You don't berate yourself for your dirty kitchen; you accept the fact that your kitchen's a little messy and you clean it up.

What can you do? Working *with* the skittish voice for a while, and acknowledging your fears and concerns stops them screaming for your attention, which in turn helps you move beyond them. Once and for all.

Sounds brilliant, doesn't it? But how do you accomplish all these wonderful things and still have time to go to work, see your friends and feed the cat?

Enter tapping.

The rock star of 'getting on with it'

Tapping is the rock star of 'getting on with it'. So what is tapping exactly? You use the fleshy pad of your fingertips to tap on designated acupressure meridian points on your body. (See diagram of acupressure points on p.51). This simple tool transmits a 'switch it off' message to the part of your brain that sends those 'wee-wa wee-wa wee-wa!' distress signals throughout your nervous system when thoughts that aren't working for you start twirling around in your head. It's the best way I've found to execute a quick turnaround in my thoughts and feelings when they're going where I don't want them to.

Tapping (also known as the emotional freedom technique, or EFT) has been around for over three decades and thanks to some dedicated scientists and practitioners it's now getting the recognition it deserves. They've been doing their best to make sure everyone knows about it *because it works*. From everything related to healing serious emotional trauma and post-traumatic stress syndrome to anxiety and phobias, it's been proven to help rewire neural pathways and rejig the 'fight or flight' response to ensure fewer trips down Pain Highway. (You can read more about this in 'Appendix 1: The science behind *Unsingle*').

The results of one tapping experiment, a highly regulated double-blind study, were so dramatic that the lab processing the results kept running and re-running the tests, assuming there was something wrong with their equipment because the decrease in stress hormones in such a limited time period was unheard of and unprecedented. All from tapping on a few points on the face and body. Pretty impressive, huh?

Tapping is extremely effective and one of the primary reasons I was able to go from single and sick of it to loved up and engaged to the love of my life within five months. It's that good. It moved my mind from the 'love is a risky business' zone into the 'love is safe and a very good idea' arena in record time. It gave my unsingling some grit and some momentum to cleave those old, cruddy ideas about love outta there. Step 1 and Step 2 prepared the way for me. Step 3, right here, is where the rubber hit the road and things really started cooking.

So let's get to it.

There are a number of different methods and uses for tapping. The one we're going to use is tapping in its simplest form – tapping around what you're thinking about. In unsingling terms this will be when you realise you're feeling anxious or unsure about life or the prospect of love.

Tapping points

On the next page is a diagram of the designated meridian acupressure points on your body. (If you'd like, go to YouTube and watch 'Unsingle's Tapping into Love' video to give you an idea of how the process works before you begin.)

Some practitioners advocate assigning a number (0 to 10) to rate the intensity of the feeling (e.g. fear of getting hurt) before and after you do your tapping, so that you can recognise if anything has shifted. For example, when you start you might rate your fear of getting hurt as a '7'. After you've tapped through a sequence, you feel the fear has eased and you'd now put the fear at a '3'. Personally, this doesn't work for me. I've never really been comfortable putting numbers on things so I don't use it. You'll need to see what works for you. They also preface teaching clients about tapping with a 'this may seem a little odd at first' speech, and they're right. It does feel a bit off-beat when you first start. But go gently, stick with it and, in my experience, the results should speak for themselves.

How to tap

The technique is very simple. You tap lightly and rhythmically with the pads of your fingertips on each of the acupressure points in the diagram, working from one acupressure point to the next sequentially. The sequence begins with tapping at what's known as the karate chop point on your hand. Think of the karate chop point as the introductory speaker. It starts the show but then leaves the stage for the main players – in this case your eyebrow through to top of your head in the order listed here. When you do more than one round, in more advanced tapping, you go back to the eyebrow point and work through the sequence again.

So, start tapping at your karate chop point (on either hand – whichever you prefer) then move through the sequence as follows:

1) **inner eyebrow**
2) **side of eye**
3) **under eye**
4) **under nose**
5) **chin**
6) **collarbone**
7) **upper side**
8) **top of head**

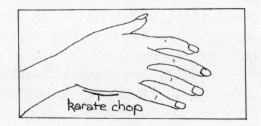

karate chop

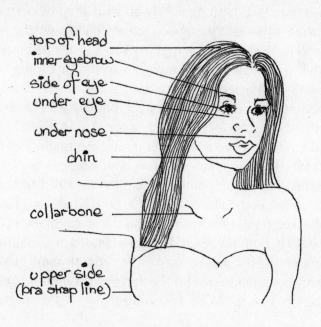

top of head
inner eyebrow
side of eye
under eye
under nose
chin
collarbone
upper side
(bra strap line)

Tapping phrases

As you tap you make a statement (known as the set-up statement) about how you are feeling – this is to be said out loud.

Before we start, let's just take a look at how thoughts can often run through our minds. We've established that tapping is here to help clear any blocks to love you may be experiencing. For example, if you have the very common fear of getting hurt, your thoughts, when you tune in and become aware of them, might go something like this: 'I'd love to have my own personal happily ever after.' Then almost immediately, the door in your mind swings back and smacks you from behind: 'But things don't always work out. What if I get hurt? I've been hurt before. I couldn't stand to go through all that again.' Your brain seizes on this thought and off you go. Before you spin off into the stratosphere terrorising yourself with alarming 'what if?' scenarios, you start tapping lightly on your acupressure points.

During a basic tapping sequence you repeat the set-up statement as you tap each point. The set-up statement we are going to use is: 'Even though I'm scared of getting hurt, I deeply and completely accept myself.' You might like to use one hand and tap on one side of the body – whichever hand and whichever side feels most comfortable. Or after you've finished tapping your karate chop point, you might like to use both hands to tap simultaneously on both sides of your face and body. When I started tapping I used only one hand and tapped one side of my body. These days I use both hands and tap both eyebrows, etcetera, because I've found the effect can be stronger. Feel free to try both single- and double-handed tapping through a sequence and see what works best for you. If you'd like to try doing it in front of a mirror for the first few attempts, to get used to the action, that might be a good idea.

So let's begin ...

1. Tap with the fingertips of one hand onto the karate chop point of your other hand, saying the set-up statement: 'Even though I'm scared of getting hurt, I deeply and completely accept myself.' Continue tapping and repeat the statement: 'Even though I'm scared of getting hurt, I deeply and completely accept myself.' Then repeat the tapping and statement a third time.

2. Move your fingertips to the inner part of your eyebrow and tap gently and repeatedly: 'Even though I'm scared of getting hurt, I deeply and completely accept myself.'

3. Now move to the outer eye, tapping lightly: 'Even though I'm scared of getting hurt, I deeply and completely accept myself.'

4. Next, tap lightly under the eye along the eye socket bone: 'Even though I'm scared of getting hurt, I deeply and completely accept myself.'

5. Now tap between the nose and the upper lip – tap, tap, tap: 'Even though I'm scared of getting hurt, I deeply and completely accept myself.'

6. Move to the crease in your chin. Keep tapping: 'Even though I'm scared of getting hurt, I deeply and completely accept myself.'

7. Tap on your collarbone. Tap a little harder here if you like: 'Even though I'm scared of getting hurt, I deeply and completely accept myself.'

8. Then tap your upper side, where your bra strap sits: 'Even though I'm scared of getting hurt, I deeply and completely accept myself.'

9. Finally, tap on the top of your head: 'Even though I'm scared of getting hurt, I deeply and completely accept myself.'

Excellent work. You've completed your first basic tapping sequence. If this feels really good and you don't want to stop, keep cycling through as many times as you like.

Once you get the hang of the process you might want to expand on the points and take it to the next level.

Tapping it to the next level

More advanced tapping begins with a basic round, using the set-up statement as before, again starting with the karate chop point. Then you go more deeply into an issue that's troubling you, tapping through a round or two of your acupressure points. In the final round you work with what I call 'the resolution', coming out the other end of the issue to the sunny side of the street using positive statements that elucidate where you want to be. Let's take a look at what this deeper version of tapping looks like.

The set-up statement round

Start with the basic tapping sequence, repeating the set-up statement: 'Even though I'm scared of getting hurt, I deeply and completely accept myself.'

Deeper into the issue round

In this round you skip the karate chop point and begin with the inner eyebrow. This is an example of going further into 'the fear of getting hurt'. It may not reflect exactly how you feel, but Nick Ortner, creator and author of the bestselling book, *The Tapping Solution* says that in the groups he facilitates, even tapping on someone else's issue often helps the person tapping feel better about their own 'stuff'. I've tested this out with my sisters and it worked for us. So even if this script doesn't exactly reflect your feelings, you might want to try it anyway. Alternatively, you can write your own script and replace the phrases below with your own.

Tap on the inner eyebrow: 'All this fear ...'
Tap on the outside of your eye: 'Don't want to get hurt ...'
Under your eye: 'Feel so frustrated. Disappointed too.'
Under your nose: 'Thought I was over this ...'
Crease in your chin: 'but it keeps coming back.'
Tap on your collarbone: 'More than anything ...'
Tap your upper side: 'I just want to let it go.'
Top of your head: 'I really want to move on.'

If you want to continue with this part, do a few more rounds about what's bothering you.

The resolution round

Again, there's no tapping on the karate chop point in this round. Note that a single resolution round works through each tapping point twice with a different statement each time. If you've written your own script, replace the following statements with your own.

Inner eyebrow: 'I want to start something new.'
Outside of your eye: 'Maybe I could move on.'
Under your eye: 'It's theoretically possible.'
Under your nose: 'There are good people out there ...'
Crease in your chin: 'lots of happy couples.'
Collarbone: 'I know it can happen.'
Upper side: 'To love and be loved.'
Top of your head: 'For it to last a lifetime ...'
Inner eyebrow: 'That could be me soon.'
Outside of eye: 'How amazing would that be?'
Under eye: 'I'd be so happy.'
Under nose: 'I'd be over the moon.'

Crease in chin: 'I feel better now ...'
Collarbone: 'I'm even a bit excited.'
Upper side: 'It feels good to know ...'
Top of head: 'true love's for me too.'

There's something that works about the fingertips tapping on the acupressure points while verbalising what's bothering you and saying that you deeply and completely accept yourself *anyway*. Stopping those debilitating thoughts about yourself or about the prospect of love is solid, solid gold. You might have never said anything like this to yourself in your entire life – time to start.

This process helps you stop and face the boogie man that's chasing you. It allows you to turn around and say, 'Right. Let's get this out and leave it behind.' And it's more effective than positive affirmations alone because whatever the magic is that tapping on those meridian points produces while making your 'where I'm at' statements and your 'where I want to be' statements, your limbic system calms down. It realises your survival is not in fact currently at risk and *it gets out of the way*.

When the trepidation is at bay, you free up your energy system and switches off the alarm around this belief or feeling. When this happens you are on love's superhighway and any blocks to love mysteriously begin to disappear.

At the end of this chapter we'll talk about working tapping into your daily routine. For now just know that it is the quickest way I have found to process negative issues from my past in order get to the good stuff i.e. true love.

Now that tapping has tilled the soil and prepared your love zone for major renovation it's time to move on. In the next section you'll learn techniques, favoured by one of the world's most famous scientists, to construct positive neural networks, paving the way for what is to come.

Einstein's favourite mind tool

Imagination (noun):
a) The ability to form new concepts, ideas or images of objects not present to the senses.
b) The mind's ability to be creative.

Einstein was a big proponent of imagination, as were many great inventors throughout history. They knew the power of the transformative ability that lay within. Sara Blakely is also a fan. The world's first self-made female billionaire used her imagination to go from selling fax machines door to door to inventing Spanx and building an enormous business empire from serious looking underpants. Actors like Arnold Schwarzenegger and Jim Carey used their imaginations to transition themselves from relative obscurity to worldwide fame, and I used it to meet the love of my life. People have used it for thousands of years to achieve what they want and they continue to use it because it works. It's free and available to everyone, which is particularly great.

Improving your love IQ

What we didn't know until recently is that imagination actually rewires your brain. Thanks to the neural imaging equipment now available, it's been proven that practising a skill and imagining practising a skill results in almost exactly the same restructuring of the related neural pathways (you'll learn more about this in Appendix 1). Dr Joe Dispenza, bestselling author of *Evolve Your Brain* puts it like this:

> *If you can influence your brain to change before you experience a desired future event, you will create the appropriate neural circuits that will enable you to behave in alignment with your intention before it becomes a reality in your life. Through your own repeated mental rehearsal of a better way to think, act or be, you will 'install' the neural hardware needed to physiologically prepare you for the new event … If so, your brain is no longer a record of the past, but has become a map of the future.*

So what does this mean to unsinglers?

Active imagining does a lot towards shifting your mind into the love zone. It feels so powerful because it is powerful. The processes you'll learn here will get your love groove going as if the person of your dreams is already in the picture. You improve your love IQ *while you're still single* because your imagination begins to restructure the neural net in your brain associated with love and relationships, making it seem utterly normal and inevitable, the next logical step in your life. A brilliant and most welcome result.

Imagine that!

'When I was twenty, I saw myself talking to Oprah,' Sara Blakely has been quoted as saying. She went on to say that, during that imagined conversation she had no idea what she was discussing with daytime entertainment's queen, just that she had achieved something Oprah would be interested enough in to put on her show. She continued visualising as she developed her company, and when Sara sent Oprah a gift basket containing the first Spanx shapewear product, it turned out Oprah was also interested enough to put Blakely's product on her body. And from what Ms Winfrey says, she has worn them almost every day since. In fact, Oprah loved them so much she broke protocol and put Sara on her 'Oprah's Favourite Things' annual show, rating Sara's invention as her number one favourite thing for the year. The show generally only features products, not people, but Oprah loved Sara's spirit and her story and decided to give her a break. Sara's vision came true. Her mental snapshot came to life. One billion dollars later, Sara's a very satisfied visualiser.

On a much smaller scale, my preferred visualisation scenario was of going to my favourite weekend getaway with my love. I couldn't picture the scene every time I tried, so sometimes I'd read the script and enjoy imagining without the associated visions of the great time we were having. Three weeks into our relationship, my husband-to-be surprised me with a trip there despite the fact that in the excitement of our first weeks together *I hadn't ever mentioned it to him.* Not once. And as it was a four-hour drive to get there it wasn't the most obvious choice for him when planning a couple of days away. The weekend was a dream come true — literally. Even better than my imaginings.

Moral of this story: the power of this process has not been exaggerated.

Your true love list

You didn't think you were going to get through a book about finding true love without making a list did you? Thankfully it's not a list of required qualities in your mate, which isn't necessary. I can't tell you how many lists I'd made over the years, trying to pen the exact description of the perfect person for me. To make things more interesting all the relationship experts who suggested writing said lists warned in a doomsday voice that you had to be extremely specific and very, *very* careful what you wished for and not to leave anything out. I still remember the angst of writing those lists – the stress! The sweaty palms, the heart palpitations, terrified I'd miss something out or get something wrong.

Let me put your mind at rest: you cannot get *this* list wrong. This list is about engaging your imagination and starting to have some fun, envisaging having someone to do things with and who adores you just as you are. It's about getting those neural nets humming with good love 'ju-ju' and positive vibes.

You're in a space now where you can utilise the relief from tapping through what's been holding you back and use that momentum, that more relaxed, open feel to write out the sort of experiences you'd like to have with your person *as if he is already here*. You'll create your true love list from things you already know you want in a relationship – yes please! And also from the things you've learnt you definitely don't want – no thanks!

The first step is to identify what goes on each list, so get a pen and paper or sit in front of your computer. An example might be:

Yes please! I'd love someone to go to Europe with: cobbled streets, fireplaces, the entire postcard deal.

No thanks! My ex never turned up to my work functions. He'd say he would come, then back out at the last second, leaving me humiliated and looking foolish in front of my boss.

Your next step is to create positive statements around these experiences. Make sure you word these experiences in the present tense, as if they are happening in the here and now. Your No Thanks! experience is flipped to the positive present tense, making it a Yes Please!:

Yes please! We're in Europe together and it's amazing. The cobbled streets, the fireplaces. It's so romantic. This place is a postcard come to life.

No thanks! (flipped to Yes Please!) My partner comes to all my work functions with me, even the really boring ones. He makes such an effort. He really is my best friend.

This is where you can give your imagination free rein. Keep adding to your list if new thoughts occur to you. I highly recommend including everyday scenarios as well as the fab overseas trips. Why? Because you need true love to feel amazing yet ordinary and everyday – this is what you want wired in.

It can also be fun to extend a point on your true love list and turn it into a five-minute mini movie, a true love script, writing yourself into a scenario of your perfect life with you in the starring role. Give it as much detail and colour as you can. Don't worry about perfect grammar. Concentrate on creating something that feels really good to you. These scripts will be at hand to use as inspiration for your visualisations in the next section, and we will incorporate both your true love list and scripts into your daily routine at the end of this chapter.

Visualisation

For some of you, visualisation will be as natural as breathing. You will close your eyes and the scene you want to picture will unfold in your mind's eye with very little effort. For others (like me) your ability to visualise will come and go and a little more effort is required to picture what you desire. You can imagine the scene by thinking, reading or writing about it when you please, you can *feel* it, but the associated visual images aren't always to hand. And then there are the non-visualisers – people who can't seem to evoke mental pictures on demand, no matter how hard they try. They read books and are transported via words into another world. Their imagination might be strong but when it comes to visualising the images just don't come.

It took me quite a few attempts to develop the ability to visualise. I'd tried many times in the past and it just hadn't happened. However, I was very interested in unsingling myself and I thought it might help, so I decided to try it one more time. Through trial and error I came up with something that worked for me and maybe it will work for you too. My ability to visualise began to emerge on a part-time basis. Perhaps like me, to be able to visualise you just need a little practice, a little patience and a step-by-step guide.

A 'snapshot' or 'glimpse' guide to visualisation

Let's go through a visualisation now. If visualising doesn't come easily to you, you'll need to make some time to take a breath and settle yourself before you begin. You might want to sit in your lounge room with all distractions switched off, or propped up in your bed in a comfortable position, again with all distractions silenced. We'll start with what I call a 'snapshot' or a 'glimpse' because it's brief and relatively simple but still very powerful. This was the way I trained my mind to start to visualise. I knew the scene I wanted to imagine so I broke it down into snapshots then joined them together. It took a couple of weeks for me to be able to properly envision the relatively simple scene that follows, but with practice I managed to get my inner television screen working.

In the future, you'll pick a scenario from your true love list or script, something personally meaningful to you, but for the purpose of illustration we'll imagine something I think every unsingler will relate to.

- Let's say you want someone to sit by you, someone to talk to and watch television with as you wind down from your day. Close your eyes, take a breath and picture yourself sitting quietly on your couch. It doesn't matter if you just get a vague outline or the picture flashes across your internal screen but doesn't remain. This is about training your mind to bring up visuals on cue. Generally, the more you practise the longer the vision will remain.
- Now picture someone right next to you, holding your hand. That's it? That's it. It can literally be a split second, a mental impression that you momentarily glimpse but it's enough to get a sense of having that person there with you, of feeling coupled up. If you think it will make it easier, you can go and look at your lounge to get the picture going in your mind, or sit on it and do your visualising from there. You can even put your hand out and rest it beside you, palm up, and with your eyes closed imagine a warm, strong hand taking yours. Wrap your fingers around the hand and just let yourself feel loved. Sometimes doing the physical action can help the mental picture come along. Even if it doesn't, it still feels pretty nice! (We'll talk more about using the 'acting as if' process later in the chapter.)
- You can stick with this same glimpse for as long as you need to, until the picture comes fairly easily to mind. It might take a week of practising for five minutes every day.
- When the image of you sitting with your love begins to feel more accessible and easier to call up, you may want to up the ante and add more detail. You might decide to picture the same scene and add your true love handing you a cup of tea, dropping a kiss on your shoulder, sitting next to you and settling down to watch your favourite show with you. In doing so you've achieved something: you've added movement to the scene and managed to envision more than you did before.
- Once that scenario feels comfortable add a little more content. Imagine sipping your tea after he's kissed your shoulder, then picture

telling him about your day as he sits quietly and listens, giving you his full attention.

You're building up the scene by gradually adding more movement and detail into the visualisation. Progress can be amazing when you allow yourself the luxury of gradual improvement.

You may have had an integrated internal movie playing in your head or a series of sequential glimpses or snapshots. Whatever works for you is fine. Just make sure you're taking the time to enjoy and magnify the feelings these visions are invoking and you are on your way.

Acting 'as if'

When I was unsingling myself one of the things I was looking forward to the most about meeting my true love was the simple act of having someone to sit close to as we wound down from our day. The desire to have someone there to chat with and watch television with was a big part of my wanting someone to love, so I decided to try to visualise it. On my fourth day of visualisation, after having had limited success, it occurred to me that perhaps doing a physical action would help the mental pictures come more clearly. I put my hand out next to me and imagined a warm, strong hand taking mine. Then I wrapped my fingers around and gently squeezed, and I was stunned by how powerful it felt and how well it worked. After a long time of being and feeling alone I was suddenly suffused with a sense of ease and comfort. It was as if I'd suddenly *let* myself feel loved. There's no other way to describe it. Even though the vision didn't come that day, I wasn't fussed. The experience had left me feeling so good, the fact I hadn't visualised even crossed my mind.

From then on, when visualising wouldn't come after reading a script I'd just sit and get the sense of how wonderful everything I'd written about would feel, imagining it was happening there and then. One of my favourite scripts was of going to my favoured weekend place with my love. When the mental pictures wouldn't come I'd close my eyes, put my hand out beside me and imagine holding my love's hand over the centre console of his car as we drove out of town for a weekend away. I'd get a sense of the music playing, of our quiet chatter and our comfortable silences and the cocooning effect of the car. It worked so well and felt so real it was astonishing. It shifted my mind to feeling that love was right next to me. And it was this scenario that materialised a few weeks into my relationship with my husband. My 'acting as if' weekend away with my love, which I had not spoken of to anyone, literally came true.

You might have a script with which you would like to try this too, even if visualisation comes easily to you. Perhaps you've written a scenario where you are at an outdoor concert. Close your eyes and sense having your true love by your side. Imagine you're both lying on a blanket. Prop yourself up on your elbows and imagine he's doing the same beside you and your arms and shoulders are touching. Imagine the music, his body's warmth and the beauty of the evening and of being outside. Sense it. Act 'as if'. Something as simple as propping yourself up on your elbows can really help prompt your imagination and give you a sense of being there. Sometimes it's just as evocative as a visual cue or visualisation would be.

Visualisation or 'acting as if' – which is better?

Is visualisation more powerful than 'acting as if'? No. They're just different.

To give you a perspective on both of these methods, imagine you've lost your keys. (Keep in mind that memory is partly a function of your imagination, because you're picturing or remembering something that is not in front of you right now.) A born visualiser would close their eyes and try to picture where they'd left their keys, whereas an 'acting as if' aficionado would immediately start thinking it through: 'I came in the front door. I put my coat down. I went to the bathroom. No, hang on a minute, I went to the laundry to check if the clothes were dry, then I went to the bathroom.' Sometimes while they're thinking they'll get up and start walking around to retrace their steps, hoping the action will prompt their memory.

'Acting as if' can simply mean thinking through an imagined scenario. Sometimes you use action to prompt your imagination, like putting your hand out or propping yourself up on your elbows as mentioned in the previous examples. What I'm saying is, either is fine. Both are equally effective. It's comparable to being either left-handed or right-handed. Visualisation is guiding your mind to picture what you want. The 'acting as if' method guides your thinking to imagine what you want. Sometimes you'll use small actions to help evoke the sense of having what you want there and then. Sometimes your thoughts are powerful enough to do that on their own (I'll talk more about this in the next chapter). Either method will help realign your neural pathways with love.

Feel your way

The best yoga teacher I ever had used to tell us time and again as she watched us straining to get into position, our faces contorted into very un-yogic like expressions: 'This is not a competition. Those of you only able to do a quarter of the pose may be doing far better than those in full lotus. That's the true practice and art of yoga.'

She was referring to the alignment and intent behind the action being the most critical thing. And that principle applies here. If a glimpse or sense of a loving partner holding your hand is all you can manage, then within that simplicity you are likely to be just as close as anyone to aligning yourself with the essence of true love. Visualisation is so powerful because of the feeling it evokes, not the ability to create visions or pictures in your mind. It's the *feeling* these visions bring up within you, of being loved and of having what you want, that turns the key. Remember, no-one is going to grade you on your visualisations, your 'acting as if', your scripts or treasure map or app. Their sole purpose is to make you feel happy, loved up and supported on your way to unsingling yourself. They're designed to bring the feeling of the love you desire right up next to you, making it seem normal and accessible and part of your everyday experience. Because *that feeling* is what flips the switch and turns the key.

So how are you going to use these processes and incorporate them into a daily practice?

Daily routine

Dedicate a fifteen-minute period once a day to focusing on moving your mind into the love zone. Last thing at night is when your mind is particularly receptive, but if a morning routine suits you better that's fine too – it's completely up to you. Apart from that, there's not a lot of wriggle room here. Unless something urgent comes up you need to maintain this practice to entrench these new thought processes. The aim is to get these new neural pathways – associating love with happiness and a place to have needs met – humming as quickly, smoothly and definitively as possible. And an established routine is the best way to achieve that. Plus it feels amazing and is fun!

Here's a quick guide:

• Sit propped up on your bed or in a chair, wherever you're most comfortable. Take a deep calming breath and feel yourself settle. Tune into any blocks that might have come up during the day (fear of getting hurt, fear of missing out, impatience, concern that you're not doing your unsingling 'right') and tap through them to a more positive place. Tapping's a lovely way to get those positive affirmations of where you want to be wired in. Or you might simply be feeling a bit wistful or tired – use that as your set-up statement e.g. 'Even though I feel a bit tired I deeply and completely accept myself.' The statement doesn't have to be directly related to love and relationships; it's also a way to process any emotion, sending a calming signal to your nervous system, soothing you and setting the scene for positive neural change.

• Next, gaze at your treasure map and enjoy seeing yourself surrounded by all the love and the great things you desire. Delight in it.

• Now read through your true love list or choose a script imagining you have someone amazing to do these things with now. Enjoy it. Take pleasure in feeling so loved. If you've tried visualisation and it's not for you, read through your list or script a few more times to get those feelings of being loved really flowing. Integrate 'acting as if' if it fits and is appropriate.

• If visualisation works for you, close your eyes and start to envision your favourite scenario or snapshot. Again, make sure you're *feeling* the feelings this imagining invokes. Really feel the comfort, the happiness, the safety, the pride, whatever emotion relates to the scenario. For example: cosying up together watching television = comfort and safety; partner making a huge effort to support you at a work function = happiness and pride.

When you're done, open your eyes, and take another deep breath. Chances are the feeling of heightened wellbeing will linger and go with you into your day or enter your dreams.

Consistency is vital when doing these practices, so make a commitment to yourself to perform them *every day*. Obviously things come up and there may be times when you have to skip a session, but I'd urge you to minimise those times whenever possible. If you need to lose half an hour of sleep, don't worry – the benefits will far outweigh any lost snooze time. You may find some days easier than others, so if you have a morning or evening where you simply can't settle, just do some tapping on whatever's on your mind then read your list or script a couple of times and spend a few extra minutes looking at your treasure map or app. Picture a snapshot or a glimpse if you can, or incorporate a little 'acting as if'. Momentum is key.

Flipping the switch checklist

♥   Time to go inside. Tapping is an important tool to add to your unsingle belt and is a mix of modern psychology and ancient Chinese acupressure. It brings the negative out into the open. Rather than keeping you stuck and scared, acknowledging how you are feeling actually helps the fear go away.

♥ Tapping is the shortest, sharpest way I've found to turn off the fight or flight response, which is one of the biggest blocks to positively rewiring and retraining your brain for love. It has been scientifically proven to dramatically decrease stress hormone levels.

♥   Imagination rewires your brain, and active imagining shifts your mind into the love zone. It feels so powerful because it *is* powerful. The processes you've learnt in this chapter will get your love groove going as if the person of your dreams is already there. You improve your love IQ *while you're still single* because your imagination begins to restructure the neural net in your brain associated with love and relationships, making it seem utterly normal and inevitable – the next logical step in your life.

♥   Create a true love list starting with a 'yes please!' and 'no thanks!' list then flipping each point into a positive, present-tense statement. Take any point and expand on it, writing a script about exactly how you would like it to play out, in the present tense as if it already is.

♥   If you're a visualiser, you'll use your scripts as an entrée into creating the cinematic version of your script. These visualisations will include everyday situations and special events but will all be based on what you are looking forward to with regards to love, making it feel very special while simultaneously seeming utterly normal.

♥ Some people's visualisations will go on for an extended period of time; some will be a five-second glimpse, a snapshot. Both are valid. Visualisation is so powerful because of the feeling it evokes not the ability to create visions or pictures in your mind. The most important thing is that you feel good and feel loved. Each person's experience will be slightly different.

♥ If you find you cannot visualise, spend the time reading your true love list and looking at your treasure map, imagining conversations you'd have and enjoying the feelings of love, anticipation and expectancy. Think about how fantastic it's going to be to have your dream partner right there beside you. Let your thoughts lead you to those wonderful feelings and enjoy them.

♥ You might want to incorporate 'acting as if' into your daily routine. After reading a script, close your eyes and prompt your imagination by a small physical action that fits in with the scene.

♥ Make a time, once a day to dedicate to these processes. Last thing at night is often best as this is usually when your time is your own and you're free from distractions. Start by gazing at your treasure map or app then read and enjoy your true love list, then one of your scripts. Use that script as a prompt to your visualisation or 'acting as if'. Consistency is important, so make a commitment to yourself and keep it. Those neural pathways aren't going to rewire themselves without input from you. Momentum is vital.

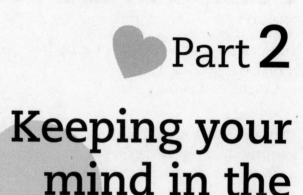

Part **2**

Keeping your mind in the love zone

Step 4
Bumps in the road

Love, like a river, will cut a new path whenever it meets an obstacle.
— Crystal Middlemas

Here you are, somewhere in the middle of your unsingling journey. You're getting the hang of the processes and getting into a groove. You don't want to jinx anything but things are going extremely well. Your daily routine is giving you more peace of mind and optimism than you've felt for quite some time. Maybe ever. Life is good and you know that soon, it's going to get even better …

Then something unforeseen happens. It catches you off guard. You hit a snag. A bump in the road. And you start to wobble alarmingly. The negative thoughts come back, thick and fast. Your resolve and belief start to crumble. You're heading straight for your love zone and a major crash looks imminent. You close your eyes and wait for the impact.

However they present and whatever they are, these bumps in the road can start those 'love is pain' pathways humming again. Without warning you're sucked back into that quagmire of negativity with the ground disappearing under your feet faster than you can stop it. They can be anything from an invitation to yet another function where you will be the only single person attending, to being ambushed at a family event with unrelenting questions as to why you're not married yet. Or maybe you ran into an ex with his new girlfriend, then your best friend called to tell you she's engaged or having a baby. Whatever the cause, it has made your stomach plummet to your shoes. You can't believe how quickly all your good work dissipates and the old 'love is for other people' mantras begin their internal chanting again. It seems everything you've done is for nothing. Your efforts have fallen short and you're back to square one.

Firstly and most importantly you need to know that this sort of thing is completely normal. Unless you have ensconced yourself in a Buddhist temple on a mountain top in Tibet for the duration of your unsingling process, you are going to be living in the modern world throughout. And as such you will encounter circumstances that challenge your belief that true love is on its way to you. It's not a sign that anything is wrong; it's part of living in society. And luckily I have a solution that I'm confident will get you through challenging times, a lifeline I used to strengthen my resolve and belief.

Thankfully this step builds on the previous ones very nicely and will help you get through the tricky times unscathed. More than that, it increases your feeling that someone to love you is on their way and takes your belief to the next level. It's a portable tool for your unsingling belt, a travelling support system that goes wherever you go and will never let you down. And its benefits are immediately apparent.

The faith wobble

Let's say the event that caused your faith wobble was receiving an invitation to a function where you will know very few people and you really, really don't want to go. There's nothing like an invitation to a five-hour long event where you'll hardly know anyone to remind you of your singleness with a resounding thud. Much as your optimism and feel-good factor have been at an all-time high this invitation manages to pierce through your newly formed layers of enthusiasm and strike you in a particularly sensitive spot. The truth is you're sick of going to functions solo; you feel like you've been doing it for years. You're tired of pasting on a smile and being polite and charming and interested when you feel anything but. And you have a sinking feeling you'll be the only single person there. The thought fills you with dread but there's nothing you can do. You have to attend. And your routine that is giving you such comfort and belief can't come with you so you have to soldier on alone. Or so you thought.

Let's play out this scenario imagining you have received the dreaded invitation and have no choice but to attend.

'The chicken or the fish?' or the last single person on Earth

The evening in question arrives and as you haven't been struck down by a life-threatening illness you reconcile yourself to a night of pretending you don't feel like the last single person on Earth. And when you arrive, stretched smile firmly in place, it's even worse than you'd imagined. In fact it's like a scene from Dante's Inferno. The bit where he's in hell.

The hosts are busy and the other people you vaguely know haven't arrived yet so you bounce rather hopelessly from group to group, smiling and nodding until your hair hurts. Your small talk seems to have dried up and, quite unusually for you, no-one seems interested in having a chat. Maybe they sense your malaise, thinly disguised behind your banter. Whatever it is, it's horrible. You don't know when you've ever felt so alone.

When you sit down to eat you don't know anyone at your table. As the courses progress, apart from the initial hellos, no-one speaks to you except the waiter, who wants to know if you'd like the chicken or the fish. You're starting to wonder if you're in fact asleep and just having a brutish nightmare. You give yourself a furtive pinch and realise this is happening. A lump forms in the back of your throat and by the time the desserts arrive it seems to have completely closed over, and you're finally glad no-one's speaking to you because you're scared if you open your mouth you'll start to cry.

You get up from the table and go outside to the deck, hoping the fresh air will soothe you. There is already a couple sitting on the bench seats on the other side, but thankfully they take no notice of you. You couldn't make polite conversation to save yourself. The positivity and optimism you've been enjoying since you started your unsingling have completely disappeared.

With your lower lip quivering like a chihuahua you are going down for the third time when a thought occurs to you, out of nowhere. Pretend he's here. Your brimming tears evaporate almost instantly. The thought is intriguing enough to interrupt your misery. You turn it over in your mind and the more you think about it the more you like it. What's to stop you morphing your 'acting as if' technique into your everyday experience, integrating it into your life? You've gotten pretty good at having conversations with your love about music and movies and the like within the realms of your imagination at home. Those daydreams, as you sit propped up in bed, and the scenarios you play out within your mind are becoming so real you feel, for the most part, that you already have a relationship that works. Before this invitation totally derailed you, you felt it was only a matter of time before he appeared in your life.

So you begin a little apprehensively. You imagine he's sitting next to you, and that his hand is rubbing your lower back in a sweet, intimate gesture. You imagine talking about nothing much. How the roast potatoes from the meal could have been used for target practice they were so hard, and how much you're looking forward to going home and sitting in bed together with cups of tea, watching your favourite show. The usual couple's chitchat when they're at a duty-bound event. It rolls out like one of your scripted scenarios and to anyone observing they would simply see a woman sitting quietly on her own.

The difference is inside you. The power of this process is formidable. You feel like a different person. It's managed to accomplish what just minutes ago you would have said was impossible. It morphed you from utter misery to real delight (and brought palpable relief) within seconds. In fact, you feel amazing! Not just a little bit better or okay, but light as air and supremely, incandescently happy. Simply because you created the feeling that you had someone there with you, someone to sit by you and laugh with. A best friend. You found a way to stop yourself falling back into old negative thought patterns about lack of support and needs never met the minute life threw you a curve ball. Instead you flipped the switch and aligned yourself with feeling loved, cared for and supported in circumstances guaranteed to push your buttons and challenge everything you've been working on. And it wasn't hard. In fact, it was spectacularly easy. And there wasn't a soul at the event that would be any the wiser. Now you can feel what it's going to be like to have someone with you at these sort of things. You know how good and how loved you will feel.

Retrograde move halted. Your love zone? Still intact. Your unsingling? Back in business.

Persistence makes the heart grow stronger

One of the things life has taught me is that if you want something, often you have to 'decide' on it more than once. You need to make the decision over and over again until whatever you've decided on turns up in your life. When everything's going smoothly your decision isn't challenged. Everything flows. You know what you want is coming to you in good time and all is well in the world. When you hit a bump in the road, a challenge, you're called on to revisit your goal and remake your decision.

Problems promote questions. Doubts. Qualms. Uncertainties. Changing those neural pathways starts immediately but it takes time to entrench the new ones and it can be a bit of a bumpy ride along the way. If you ever find yourself flagging and feel like you need a bit of a rev up, you can turn to classic texts like Napoleon Hill's *The Master Key to Riches*, one of the bestselling books of all time. One of the riches he consistently talks about throughout his book is love. Hill is strong and definite, and books like his can be intimidating, particularly for us females who often pride ourselves on being flexible (and we should be proud of it; it's an admirable trait). But there are times when flexibility can actually mean we're chickening out by not putting our foot firmly down and standing by our decisions.

Sometimes life requires an answer from us. It requires us to shift ourselves out of neutral, to make up our mind and continue to make decisions that support our original choice until what we want appears in our life. Goethe told us, 'Boldness has genius, power and magic in it.' And it does. Fortune favours the brave. So does love.

It would be wonderful if whatever we decided upon turned up immediately, directly in front of us. We all secretly long for that sort of life. But living requires a certain amount of courage and determination. And although no-one wants problems or challenges they can help us. They push us to learn things about ourselves and grow stronger and more determined if we don't let them roll over us. They can teach us persistence and tenacity. They help us understand that if we want something we have to show up to accept it. But if we're still dithering back at the fork in the road, how are we ever going to get where we're headed to receive it?

Letting fear go, letting love in

As you know, unsingling is about bringing the feeling of love right next to you, making it seem ordinary and every day. This practice of integrating visualisation and 'acting as if' into everyday events and real life is like a rehearsal of your future, of what you will have. If you have trouble visualising, concentrate on feeling supported and just imagine a conversation, like the one referred to in the example, that you might have with your love in the setting without trying to conjure up the associated mental pictures. This step is important, so make sure you use it in either form, when it feels right. It provides invisible support, keeping your mood happy and upbeat while reducing any fear you might have about how you will handle it when your wishes actually come true.

It sounds silly, but sometimes we greatly fear getting what we want the most. Depending on how long you've been single, you will have some reservations about falling in love, even though it's what you want so much. You might be scared of it never happening for you and about how you will handle it if it does. You might start to wonder if you know how to 'do' relationships and doubt whether you'll know how to behave. You get nervous about messing it all up. You won't. Well actually, you will mess a few things up, and so will he. Luckily that's all part of it. But any fear you're carrying can keep love at arm's length.

Incorporating visualisation or 'acting as if' techniques into your daily life can, I believe, help quieten those fears and give you a dry run to get your head around the fact that the person you're going to meet will become one of your best friends. And there's nothing scary about him at all. He's actually pretty wonderful and he thinks you're wonderful and you both think the other is the bee's knees, the cat's pyjamas, the dog's whiskers and any other superlative you can think of. These processes can help you to quit worrying and know this extraordinary relationship is what you deserve.

Staying in the love zone

There are so many ways you can use this real time imagining, and if you decide to use it you'll have a lot of fun. It can be integrated into just about any setting you desire and it serves particularly well any scenario you're nervous about or that causes you anxiety.

But it doesn't have to be restricted to Code Red situations. Any time you think it will settle you is a good time to use it. Perhaps you've been at work all day and you've come home, eaten dinner and are sitting down to watch television. You've had a busy day and are looking forward to zoning out and not thinking about anything much. You feel okay, but there's a slight wistfulness floating around the edges of your consciousness. Before long you notice you're wishing you had someone there with you. Instead of letting your mind take a stroll down Slightly Sad and a Bit Lonely Street, click into imagination mode, imagining he's sitting beside you quietly holding your hand. Or lean back into the cushions and sense you're resting against his chest, feeling his arms wrap around you. Just get the feeling of that comfort, safety and security. Let the calming effect of having someone who thinks you're wonderful sitting close by soothe you. Keep watching the television and enjoy the experience. You're imagining a very simple and commonplace activity but it can help you reap huge psychological benefits. It stops you from concentrating on the feeling of lack and blowing it up into something it's not. It keeps you focused on the fruition of your dreams, not on the notion that your love hasn't arrived yet. And it can stop you sabotaging yourself with little gremlin thoughts of impatience or dissatisfaction and disbelief. And because it's so ordinary it seems achievable. You're training your mind away from the idea that love is this daunting prospect, reminding you how wonderful and amazing it is, and again bringing that feeling of love right up next to you.

So practise the feeling of having your love with you whenever you want. As with your 'yes please!' and 'no thanks!' list, with its positive and negative connotations and motivations, the times you decide to use this technique can vary. It can be used to make a happy event even happier. Or it can be when you're engaged in something you're uncomfortable with and the idea of having your love with you can flip the switch and make everything feel just fine.

You might be feeling really, really good when you walk to your corner store with your dog on a Saturday morning. The sun's out and you're revelling in an incredible lightness of being, transported by the cuteness of your canine and the luxury of a whole weekend stretched out before you. Then you think how nice it would be to have your true love there with you, the sunshine warming your backs as you walk together. So you imagine that he's with you and that you're chatting about inconsequential things. Things like remarking how good the sun feels on your skin and what you want to do for dinner tonight as you watch your dog trot and snuffle and wag her tail, having the time of her life. The conversation doesn't have to be about anything momentous or important. In fact, it's better if it's not. Ordinary and everyday is the vibe you're going for. The more normal it is, the more achievable it will feel. The more feeling associated with your thoughts and your focused attention, the stronger, faster and more definitively the associated neural pathways rewire. So a moment of simple, pure happiness projected on your internal screen can work wonders, strengthening your love zone while increasing your joy exponentially just from the idea of sharing it with someone who loves you.

On the other side of the coin you might be doing something you'd rather not be doing. You may have to attend a family function, and much as you love your family you are very much over turning up alone. Instead of walking in with your stomach in knots, imagine your love is next to you, holding your hand, giving you strength. If anyone starts haranguing you about your love life, feeling like your fellow is right there will give you confidence and you'll probably be able to let any comments about your love life float right over your head. You don't have to continue imagining all evening if you don't want to; sometimes a quick glimpse, a momentary imagining of him squeezing your hand, whispering 'Can we go home now?' is all you need to make you smile and get you through. If you want to keep it going a little longer and it gets you past the first five minutes or half an hour and you're feeling more relaxed, you can retire it for the night. Whatever you want.

These imaginings are a tool – in my experience an exceptionally amazing tool, granted, but a tool nonetheless. And what do tools do? They work for you. They're designed to help make whatever you're working on easier. As with all the other tools in your unsingling belt, this one makes your mind work for you. It keeps you in the love zone, which is exactly where you want to be. You're using your imagination every day anyway, it's just that prior to unsingling you were most likely oblivious to the process and to the fact you were often imagining the worst. This way you're retraining your brain for love and happiness, which is a far more productive use of your time and the awesome power of your mind.

The previous steps laid the groundwork and this 'acting as if' is the catalyst for what is to come. Your unsingling is well on its way and it's exciting. You've come through the challenging times unscathed. Better than that, your belief in the power of love has grown because you're letting it in more and more. And you're getting stronger. Less pulled about by what is going on around you. Allow yourself a moment of feeling quietly impressed with your progress. You deserve it.

Bumps in the road checklist

♥   You will very likely hit a few bumps in the road on your journey to unsingleness. It's perfectly normal and does not indicate you're doing anything wrong. Do your best to accept the situation that has temporarily derailed you and adapt, using, positive visualisation, 'acting as if' and imagination where possible.

♥   If you have to attend a function alone and you feel the momentum you've built up faltering, integrate your visualisation or 'acting as if' technique into the scenario and imagine you have a supportive partner by your side.

♥   If you have trouble visualising, concentrate on *feeling* supported and imagine in words a conversation you might have with your love in the setting, without trying to conjure up the associated mental pictures. (Most of us have plenty of experience of thinking what we will say to people, rehearsing in our mind the conversation we will have as part of our everyday normal mental chatter. Just tailor the mental chatter to the situation and imagine the conversation is between you and your partner.)

♥ This is about making your mind work for you. In using this method you're keeping your mind occupied and giving it something positive to do.

♥ Use this integration method in any day-to-day activity you would like to be doing with your partner. Make sure your imagined scenarios are of ordinary activities, things you would be doing together on a regular basis, so they seem real, achievable and well within reach. For example, going shopping, watching television, walking the dog, attending a family event.

♥ The purpose here is to make your relationship feel like it is right next to you, not in some far away galaxy. These scenarios will calm and soothe you, allowing you to relax while you wait for your true love partner to arrive.

Step 5
Negativity diet

To thine own self be true.
— William Shakespeare

Diets, despite their popularity, are usually associated with pain and deprivation. No-one enjoys being told they need to go on a diet and few people enjoy telling another person they need to go on one. Luckily, this isn't that sort of diet. The negativity diet is not a new concept. It refers to a complete bypassing of negative input on any subject, to increase a person's clarity and happiness quotient. Lots of self-help authors recommend it. In unsingling it's a little more specific; it strictly pertains to matters of the heart. It's about abstaining from negative *relationship* input. There may still be a few behaviours you need to modify, a few factors you're missing, saboteurs that need to be banished from your unsingling kingdom. Why? Because without you knowing it these factors could be undermining the great work you're doing. Not stopping it, but slowing it down. And you definitely don't want that.

Neurons that fire together wire together

Remember the unsingling filter we talked about in 'Step 1: Clearing the way', ensuring input is either positive or neutral when it comes to love? An extension of the books and the magazines discussed is what you watch on television. You may have already modified the programs you tune into without knowing exactly what you were doing or why. But hopefully by now you're listening more to yourself than to the outside world, noticing when something starts to bring those negative thoughts racing back. And you're making a conscious decision to not go there, removing your attention from whatever is making you uneasy.

A major part of unsingling is doing your best to create an environment around you that promotes and supports healthy relationships and love. No, you're not living on a mountain top in Tibet and you cannot control everything around you. We're talking about what you can control and, when you have the choice, removing your attention from anything that will start up those habitual negative thoughts again.

When you think the same thoughts over and over you forge a neural pathway within your brain which becomes a sort of ingrained position. It takes time to forge new ones, meaning that when something happens or when there is input that unnerves you, you often slip back into the familiar old neural net, your comfort, or more correctly your dis-comfort zone. Those neural pathways are used to being accessed. They've formed a well-worn path. What you've been doing is making a conscious effort to forge fresh neural pathways, using your visualisations and other unsingling tools to create a different set position, a new neural net within your thought processes when it comes to love. These pathways focuse on how great love is, how much fun it is, how much support and comfort being loved gives you.

Your aim is for the old neural pathways that associate love with pain to shrivel and become deactivated through lack of use. When you are retraining your brain, you need to be conscious of what you allow in. When an athlete is in training they don't feed themselves fast food. Whatever they put into their body is refined, targeted and devised specifically to ensure their efforts and hard work produces the best possible results. While unsingling isn't a sport, you are on Team Love and the same principles apply. Your mind needs a steady diet of pure, positive love input for these new neural pathways to form.

It's just a show ...

If you're watching a television show or a movie that is focused on a couple in strife – fighting, lying to one another or being unfaithful – how strong do you think your belief in true love is while you're watching it, on a scale of one to ten? I'm not talking about romantic comedies where you know everything will turn out fine in the end. I'm talking about shows that focus on the darker side of love, the sort of stuff that turns your heart icy in your chest. Probably not that strong on the love-o-meter right? If that's the case, watching it isn't working for you is it? So do yourself a favour and turn it off. Don't give those negative neural nets a reason to start pulsing again.

If you live with other people and they're watching a program that's making you uneasy, just go to your room and read for a while. Do some online browsing. Take a bath. As long as you're not giving your focused attention to love in trouble, you're doing well. You can make the decision not to go there, and don't worry if people don't understand what you're doing or think you're being odd. You don't need to explain yourself. A simple 'I'm not in the mood for this sort of thing' will suffice.

You've made the choice to unsingle yourself and find true love and you need to stick to it. If you start to explain, you start to justify and you lose ground. Announcing you don't want to watch something because it will mess with your love zone isn't necessary and will probably earn you some very strange looks. Do your own thing and let those around you do theirs. Just make sure you're doing it quietly.

On autopilot

My sister and I were talking recently about how heading down the wrong neural pathways can be habitual. She likened it to something she'd experienced during her university years. I thought it was a really good analogy so I'm relating it here.

She travelled the roads from our home to and from her college so often it was embedded into her consciousness, a learnt behaviour. It became such a habitual route that more than once she found herself automatically heading there when she was actually going somewhere else. Neural pathways for those left- and right-hand turns were deeply ingrained. This is how your habitual thoughts can work if you don't remain aware of where you want to go; you can end up in the wrong place because you've let your mind go onto autopilot.

This isn't to suggest you need to rigorously and continuously monitor every single thought you have. It just means that when you find yourself in a place you don't want to be, your mood changes, you notice it and you change direction. My sister didn't keep driving towards campus when she realised she was meant to be going elsewhere – she simply corrected her course, made the appropriate turns and got on the road she wanted to be on.

The trick here is that she became aware that she was travelling on the wrong road. Awareness is key. A good indicator or signpost that you need to change roads is *noticing when your mood has dropped.* In this way, a mood change can be a good thing and can help you, because it alerts you that you might be travelling down – and thus strengthening – the wrong neural pathway and the wrong neural net.

Music to your ears

You also need to take notice of what you're listening to on your iPod or the radio. Music affects people's spirits more quickly and often more deeply than just about anything else. But don't worry: unsingling doesn't require a *fatwa* on enjoying music. Far from it. You can and should listen to boppy songs and get your groove on whenever you feel like it, or relax to soothing tunes that make you feel good. But there needs to be a few exceptions to your listening pleasure, for the time being at least.

You've probably experienced the delicious agony of playing sad, sad songs when you've just had your heart broken or when you're single, heartsore and looking for love. Tears pouring down your face as you revel in the exquisite pain. As much as humans usually do their level best to avoid pain, for some reason, through music we're drawn to it like moths to a flame. Perhaps because it gets to us. It can stop us in our tracks and make us feel, which is not as accidental as you might suppose. Ask any composer and they will tell you the notes that are the 'sad' notes and the ones that are 'happy', and that they use them accordingly, depending on how they want the listener to respond. People who compose scores for movies are experts at it. You know just by the tone of the music playing whether the character entering the room is of pure or sinister intent. It's shorthand to your emotions.While you're unsingling the wrong kind of song can cut through layers of newly found optimism and hope very quickly if it's designed to take you to a sad place.

'Someone Like You' by Adele is one of the most beautiful, haunting songs I've ever heard. In the song she wishes her former love well with his new partner and new life, and the sorrow and poignancy are unmistakable. I distinctly remember the first time I heard it. I was shopping when it came over the store's sound system and from almost the first note I became mesmerised. I forgot where I was for a moment – quite literally – I was that enthralled. By the end of the song I had tears in my eyes, my heart was in my boots and despite being a happily married woman I felt like I'd lost something, that love equals heartbreak and nothing ever, ever turns out the way you want it to. It affected me that much. I couldn't shake the feeling for hours.

I spoke to another woman about the song later that week because I wanted to find out if other people found it equally affecting. She was a Pilates instructor and looked like she'd never had a sad day in her life. She told me that when she first heard it she was hanging out her washing and had to stop and sit down on a bench behind her because she was suddenly finding it hard to breathe. (And if you know anything about Pilates instructors, you'll know they're champion breathers.) Her answer confirmed the conclusion I'd come to, despite telling myself I'd been ridiculous and it was just a song: logic doesn't account for the way you feel. And as previously discussed, how you *feel* plays a huge part in what you draw into your experiences.

So for the purpose of unsingling and flipping the switch, please make yourself a playlist that takes you to a happy place. You can include whatever sort of music and whichever artists you like, as long as it makes you feel relaxed or 'up'. If any of your favourite artists record a miserable ballad about love not working out, you should still give it a miss. *Even* if it's the best song ever and considered cool. I love the song I just mentioned but it hasn't been added to my playlist. I made a choice. And I'm already successfully unsingled.

It's pretty simple. If your energy goes up when you listen to a particular song, its fine, keep playing it. But if you find yourself feeling down, if it reminds you of a love that ended or never began, turn it off. Enough said.

To see or not to see

While we're on the subject of cool, you may or may not be supremely groovy. You might attend the best events, have the hippest wardrobe and possess the most cutting edge tech gadgets that would make Mark Zuckerberg green with envy. And there's nothing wrong with any of that. Maintaining that status, however, can put you in a somewhat sticky position when you're unsingling yourself. If the thought of missing out on the newest cult movie that everyone's talking about makes you feel faint, but the movie is about a train crash of a relationship, you're back in the realm of choices. And you need to do what you think is best for you. You might be surprised at how liberating it feels *not to go*.

If you do decide to see it, take the time to notice how you feel either when you're sitting in the bar or café afterwards discussing it with your friends or when you get home and are on your own. If it isn't good, and if you find a certain gloom has descended when you think about love, you'll know to make a different choice next time. Don't beat yourself up for having gone.

Sometimes going against the unsingling ethos and making these sort of choices simply because you want to can be a positive thing. It throws into sharp relief what we've been talking about: that the mind often goes down the path of what it is observing and continues on ad infinitum after the stimulus has ceased. What does that mean? That watching a movie about a disintegrating relationship and its associated pain gets you thinking about the pain you've experienced in relationships. And long after the movie has finished your mind can carry on entertaining itself with terrifying 'what if?' scenarios that don't work for you. If you've been feeling a tad sceptical about the power of the mind when it comes to love, these sorts of experiences, where true love feels a million miles away again, can help put that scepticism to rest.

'Within reason'

Unsingling has a very specific focus, and you know what it is: to shift your attention from negative relationship input to concentrate on true love and happiness; harnessing the power of your constantly rewiring brain to develop positive neural associations. when it comes to love. But as previously mentioned you're not living on a mountain top in Tibet, which increases the likelihood that you will at times find yourself in situations not to your choosing but where absenting yourself would upset the status quo. So I'd like to add a disclaimer here: Remove yourself or your attention from negative relationship input within reason.

As everyone will probably have a slightly different take on what constitutes 'within reason', clarification is in order. My definition is this: If you are able to remove yourself from negative 'love' discussions or situations without causing a scene, or upsetting or embarrassing anyone (including yourself), that's fine. If not, it's often best to just sit it out.

If you would like more clarification complete this quick questionnaire:

1. You are out with friends or work colleagues for lunch and the latest break-up anthem comes over the sound system in the restaurant. Do you:

a) Run screaming from the table with your hands over your ears to wrench the stereo from the wall?

b) Remain chatting and eating and figure it will be over soon?

2. A huge marriage scandal has just hit the news and everyone is talking about it over lunch. Do you:

a) Run screaming from the table with your hands over your ears until you are safely out in the street?

b) Remain chatting and eating and figure it will be over soon?

Hopefully you answered b) to both questions! One discussion, one movie, program or song is not going to ruin all the good work you have been doing. It's not ideal, but it's not dire straits either. Don't lose any sleep over it.

Shifting your focus

If you begin to change the subject when your girlfriend starts to talk about her partner and what she perceives as his list of defects, hopefully she will take your cue and begin to talk of more pleasant things. If she doesn't get the hint, perhaps you can ask her what her favourite things about him are and what he's done recently that was kind or that made her laugh. Or remind her of a funny story that you all shared – anything to get her thinking differently will help both of you. Her relationship will benefit from her shift in focus, and you get to avoid the thoughts that come as a matter of course when talking about what is wrong, what isn't working and what needs aren't being met. At the risk of sounding like a broken record, you need to be feeding yourself a steady diet of positive love messages right now. It just makes sense.

There's no denying it can be a little tricky to navigate these changes with friends and family at first. Especially if there's been a pattern of them venting and you listening, a role single women often find themselves in. But the benefits make your efforts (and any uncomfortable pauses in conversation) worthwhile. When you begin to concentrate and focus on happy relationships, more and more examples of these types of couples will come to your attention. All of a sudden you'll find articles in magazines about how blissful two people are together and read them happily. They'll stand out to you because your unsingle filter is working on your behalf. You'll notice more couples holding hands as they walk along and you'll smile knowing soon that will be you.

You'll overhear more conversations where people are saying loving things to one another, in person or over the phone. You will become a love magnet because the more you look for, concentrate on and believe in love, the more examples will be drawn to you. And the more examples you see and hear, the stronger your belief becomes. And it all snowballs and you get a very handy cumulative effect that takes a lot of the effort from your shoulders and hands it over to love.

What you look for is what you'll find

You've probably heard the saying that what you look for you will find. You may have even had the rather unpleasant experience of meeting someone for the first time and your every word, action or look seems to annoy them. For whatever reason they've decided they dislike you and they're looking for reasons to endorse their dislike. The more you do to convince them otherwise, the clumsier and more unlikeable you become. Your actions get twisted to justify their negative opinion of you. It's horrid.

You've also probably had the opposite, far more pleasant experience of meeting someone who thinks you're wonderful.

see no negative love stuff hear no negative love stuff speak no negative love stuff

Everything you do pleases them. They think you're funny, charming, kind and generally quite lovely. Consequently you become funnier, more charming, kinder and lovelier in their presence, blossoming like a flower basking in the sun of their warmth.

It's the same with love. If you think love sucks you'll find ample reasons to justify your viewpoint. Everywhere you look you'll see examples of love gone awry. Why? Because the brain looks to match patterns it holds within itself through conditioning. But condition your mind to seek out love, give love the attention and appreciation it deserves and it will begin to show off for you. You'll be looking at the world through a different filter and love will be everywhere. You'll be focusing in on completely different things and that focus, coupled with a bit of patience, will bring you more joy, peace and happiness than you would have ever believed.

The negativity diet is about giving yourself permission to take charge of what goes in to your psyche. It's simple: if you want a relationship that is extraordinary, you have to be feeling pretty darn special. You have to make the time and space to ready yourself for someone who is going to exceed every expectation you've ever had. But if you don't make room for him by removing your headspace from the drama of the media and the people that surround you, quieting your mind enough to focus on what you want, you could block that love from flowing to you. Don't underestimate the impact of the constant stimulation our society provides. It's exciting but it can also be extremely noisy. Take a step back, decide what you want and keep focusing upon it. Where possible disengage from the drama.

It really is worth the effort.

Negativity diet checklist

♥ Habitual thoughts forge neural nets within your brain, which act like an emotional default position. Frequent negative thoughts about love and relationships mean, with very little stimulus, you find yourself recreating old emotional pain. Unsingling is all about replacing these neural nets with positive neural pathways, affirming how brilliant love is, setting a new emotional paradigm within your psyche.

♥ Thoughts and emotions tend to flow toward what you are observing. Ensure the programs and movies you watch support your goal to stay positive about love.

♥ Music plays straight to your emotions. Songs about heartbreak and loss shouldn't feature on your current playlist. If they come on the radio while you're driving either switch stations until you find an upbeat or soothing tune, or turn your radio off.

♥ Unsingling is a groove-free zone. Don't listen to things, read things, discuss things or watch things that you know aren't supportive of your goal just because they're cool. Your grooviness will still be there for you when you're successfully unsingled. But if you do listen to, watch or read something with negative themes about love, take note of how you feel afterward. If it's made you feel noticeably pessimistic or glum, this at least confirms the validity of the unsingling ethos. Take the positive lesson and move on.

♥ Don't feel the need to defend your actions to your friends and family, but don't draw attention to them either. Announcing you're not going to watch a program, don't want to see that movie or listen to that song because it will mess with your love zone is unnecessary. Just do your thing and let everyone else do theirs. Make your choices and stick to them. Quietly.

♥ What you look for is what you will find. A person who thinks love sucks will find many examples to back up their theory. But if you give love the attention and appreciation it deserves, it will begin to show off for you. You will become a love magnet and notice examples of love and loving behaviour everywhere you look.

♥ If the people around you are engaged in a conversation you know you don't want to be a part of because it goes against your renewed belief in love and having needs met, make an excuse if possible and remove yourself quickly and quietly. Don't judge the people for their topic of conversation. Give it no energy at all. Just continue to think about your true love and how much you're looking forward to meeting him.

♥ 'Within reason' means you need to use discernment to decide whether it's appropriate or not to remove yourself from negative discussions, and so on. Good manners should always be employed.

Step 6
Minding the gap

Oh give us the man who sings at his work.
— Thomas Carlyle

I once had the good fortune to work in an office opposite a small shopping centre in a suburb of Melbourne. The good fortune came not from the job but from the man who ran the grocery store I walked past every morning after parking my car. As I'd enter the centre's doors, preoccupied by whatever issues awaited me on my desk, I'd hear him singing *Don Giovanni* at the top of his lungs as he set up for the day, his voice reverberating through the empty aisles. And I absolutely loved it. Hearing his *joie de vivre* made me so happy I started to time my arrival just so I'd hear him. And I think a lot of other people did too. We'd grin at each other as we passed, soaking in the lusty vocals of a man in love with life. His high spirits helped us forget whatever issue was bothering us and *revel in the moment*. I don't know if it was his fearless delivery, his excellent voice or his Italianate style. Whatever it was, it was catching. This was a man who knew how to enjoy life. He could have lugged the boxes of fruit and veg grudgingly around his store, chuntering that Pavarotti wasn't all that great, and wasn't he just as good? But without ever really speaking to him it was obvious that wasn't his style. He exuded vibrancy and an extraordinary ability to grab life by the horns and enjoy it. I always assumed he was married. If he wasn't, he would have had women lining up to go out with him, I'm sure. Why? Because he was happy.

The charisma of a happy person is undeniable. If you walked into a packed cinema and saw a spare seat next to a relaxed, happy looking individual and another next to someone who was glowering at the world or looking anxious and miserable, where would you choose to sit? This isn't to say you need to go around with a Joker-like grin on your face to attract the love of your life, because that could be a bit scary. But happiness, the decision to – wherever possible – look for things that make you smile, can make a big difference to your day and to the energy you're putting out into the world.

'Minding the gap' is about a couple of things. Mainly it's about keeping yourself optimistic while you're waiting for your true love to show up. You've probably been doing the unsingle steps for a few months now and I'm hoping your moods have

improved and that you feel different, lighter. Those neural pathways are starting to work *for* you. The shift from helpless and hopeless to empowered and expectant is nothing to be sneezed at.

But waiting – or 'the gap' – can do funny things to people. The gap is the time and space between the change taking place inside you and the physical result appearing in your life. Just like the ebb and flow of the ocean – the intake of breath before the big exhale – there is often a space, a momentary stillness before true love arrives in your life. And during the in-breath or the ebb part of the cycle the relief you felt when you started unsingling can start to fade and give way to impatience. And impatience can lead to doubts. And doubts can lead to more doubts which, if left unchecked, can lead to giving up on the whole darn thing. Please don't. The London Underground gives good advice when they tell their passengers to 'mind the gap', referring to the space between the carriage and the platform when they're getting on or off the train. They're trying to stop people from missing their footing and sliding ignominiously between, meeting a very nasty fate.

To keep you from missing your footing and possibly falling into the gap, I'd like you to consider approaching this waiting period from a different angle. If you know any skiers you'll know how much pleasure they take in the anticipation and preparation for the season ahead. They make their preparations part of the enjoyment too. They get their gear ready, keep their eye on the weather channel and imagine how much fun they'll have at the end of the day at après-ski, drinking schnapps with their friends. They start dreaming about fresh powder and perfect conditions, the mountain air and sun on their face. Skiers don't just enjoy the ski season. They get great mileage out of the lead-up to the opening weekend and a good two extra months of enjoyment without even seeing or touching snow.

Minding the gap means taking a leaf out of the skiing fraternity's book and making the most of your prep time. Let the fizzy joy of anticipation get the better of you and instead of focusing on what isn't here yet, enjoy the lead-up to your true love show.

Shake your money maker

This is where the singing grocer comes in. You might not have his chutzpah but singing and/or shaking it – even if it's only in your bedroom, the shower or your car – can be a great way to start the day. You might also find it a good antidote to any doubt floating around the edges of your consciousness. Or if you're already feeling good, it's a nice way to ensure that once your steps are done your mind stays happy and doesn't cloud over when you think of the day ahead.

There are a couple of different ways to do this. One is to choose an upbeat song that always makes you feel good and sing that. The second is to change the words to any boppy tune you like, to suit getting your unsingling groove on. Say you're a fan of the Motown classics, like the Supremes' 'You Can't Hurry Love.' You love the music but you would like to hurry love thanks very much, so change the words to reflect what you want. Flip the switch on the lyrics and write the opposite in the present tense, first person and off you go. A perfect unsingling tune.

Your happy place

If singing is absolutely not your thing but a morning booty shake appeals, turn up the radio and start shaking it to the music of your choice. You might be the most uncoordinated dancer ever but this isn't about smooth moves. It's about moving your body and having a laugh. If you share your living space with other people, do it in the bathroom after your shower. (Just make sure the floor is dry – no skidding out of control across the tiles please!) It doesn't have to be the full whirling dervish. A couple of hip flicks and a sweeping hand across the horizon, finger pointed at your audience a la the all-girl bands of the 1960s will usually be enough to evoke a giggle, particularly if you do it facing the mirror.

You probably gave up singing into your hairbrush when you stopped putting on concerts for your parents with your bed sheet as a stage curtain. And that may or may not have been a long time ago. But whether you're seventeen or 47, resurrecting that girl will take you to your happy place and help you lighten up and not get too serious. Unsingling is a good time to reconnect with the cheerier part of yourself. You want to have fun when you're with your true love, don't you? Then start practising. And unless dancing and singing is your idea of torture, give it a try and take note of how even a few minutes in the morning increases your happiness quotient for the day.

It's another tool to put in your unsingling belt to support you wherever and whenever you need some assistance. And like most of the unsingling tools, it's portable. It can go where you go, in a slightly modified version. Just like the imagining we've talked about in previous chapters, the portable version goes on internally. Busting out your moves or bursting into song in the office when you feel you need a lift or a distraction from unwelcome thoughts won't be well regarded unless you work for a singing telegram company. But a little internal singing of a few verses of 'It Must Be Love' or similar – something sweet, upbeat and feel-good – can make a surprising difference to your mood.

Realise you're thinking about an ex that did you wrong as you wait in the queue for your morning coffee? Sing a verse or two in your head to help drown out any negativity and it will often bring you back into the present without going for the ride. Distraction works wonders on the wandering mind. Give it something else to think about, something happy and fun and it will latch onto that. It won't work every time (which we'll talk more about a little later) but more often than not it will save you. Crisis of confidence contained. Situation averted and your mood levels get back on track.

All of these suggestions are just that. They're not necessary steps so don't get yourself into a lather thinking, 'If I don't dance and sing every morning I won't meet my true love and everything will be ruined'. That is absolutely *not the case*. True love doesn't require auditions. It's not *American Idol*. If you try singing or dancing, or both, and it doesn't make you laugh or smile, it's probably best not to bother with it. The whole point is to make you relax and feel good about things; if it just makes you feel uncomfortable find something else that tickles your funny bone. Sometimes a simple 'Yay!' can keep your mood up there, particularly if the joy of your morning routine is fading and you don't want to go to work.

Another thing I used to do when I was unsingling was choose one of my favourite funny movies and put it on. I wouldn't watch the whole movie or show, I'd just fast forward to the scene that was guaranteed to make me laugh. The scene was often not more than a few minutes long but it worked every time I watched it. If you have any movies or TV shows saved or on disc and know there's a bit that makes you laugh, chortle, titter, giggle or grin, put it on in the morning before you head to work. Or if there's a clip on YouTube that you find really funny, play that to make you smile. I still do this when I need a lift and it works a treat. If I'm happy it makes me happier, and if I'm stressed laughing always calms me down.

Happiness isn't only related to laughing. Napoleon Hill says happiness is in the doing, not merely possessing. I think happiness for a lot of us is in remaining 'aware'. There are so many things we miss every day because we're on autopilot. Unsingling is a good time to take a breath and start to enjoy and appreciate the world around you. Very small things can give you pleasure when you take the time to notice them. Maybe you have a great coffee shop near your work and you treat yourself a takeaway latté every morning on your way into the office. Next time when you take a sip actually take a moment to 'taste' it. Stop pounding the pavement and let yourself pause to savour the incredible flavour. Appreciate it. What's the point of treating yourself if you don't even notice or appreciate the enjoyment you get from it?

When I was writing this book I was so focused on getting it written that I forgot to slow down occasionally and enjoy the process. I didn't have the time, I told myself. When I realised what I was doing – that I was squeezing the pleasure out of my days because I was too 'busy' – I started taking an early morning walk. I knew that my enjoyment of the beauty of a fresh morning would make me more productive and just plain happier. I'd see dogs on their walks with their owners; the joy in their every bouncy step, their exuberance, their panting smiles (and that was just the owners). There's something in that for unsinglers.

We've talked about how having this extraordinary love in your life will transform your days and increase your happiness exponentially. However, don't just practise the feeling when you're reading your scripts and doing your visualisations. Get in the groove of savouring life now. Take the time to value what you have, and you will be able to enjoy the lead-up to meeting your true love a lot more.

The 'yay!' experiment

You've probably already realised the rewiring of your neural pathways can be applied to any area of your life you wish to improve. Long before I had heard of neuroplasticity I had an experience which, now that I look back at it, makes perfect neuroscientific sense. I was sharing a house with someone and was in the aforementioned job I didn't love. My housemate and I would walk past each other in the hallway each morning on our way to and from the bathroom and greet each other with very little enthusiasm (she was also in a job she wasn't overly fond of). Somehow over time our greeting changed to an ironic 'yay' – definitely no exclamation point – making light of the fact we were less than thrilled to be going to work. For some reason the flat sounding 'yay' made us laugh, probably because such a happy word was being said in such an unenthusiastic way.

Then one morning I said, 'Why don't we do this properly? Say it as if we mean it and see how it feels?' So we tried it. Each morning the 'yay!' became progressively louder, happier and more exuberant. After a few weeks we were grinning and beaming as we did it, trying to outdo each other with how much joy we could squeeze into that one syllable. I believe we may have even integrated a few bunny hops and girly air-punches into the ritual.

The changes were visible. Our cheeks were flushed, our eyes shone and we couldn't stop smiling. Anyone watching us would have sworn we'd just received some very good news. And like a child making a toy out of scraps, we'd created our own happiness out of thin air. Nothing in our lives had changed except us. We interrupted the neural pathways that associated getting up on a weekday with gloom and decided to just get on with it and enjoy life as much as possible. We'd made the choice to be happy, to generate our own happiness. And it was easy and fun! Those glums were a habit we'd gotten into, a well-accessed neural pathway that I don't think either of us really thought about, it felt so automatic.

Seeing as the 'yay!' experiment had been such a success, I began to look for things that made me feel that way throughout the day. And as a result I started to feel lighter and happier. Soon after that I had to find a different place to park my car because the zoning behind my office block had been changed. That was when I discovered the singing grocer, and my happiness factor increased again. Not long after that I got a promotion to a job I really liked and a swish new car to drive to work, which all contributed to me feeling even more sparky. All of a sudden I had *plenty* to cheer about.

Would I have chosen to park in the shopping centre and discovered the singing grocer had we not started the 'yay!' experiment? I don't know. Would I have received the promotion that made me love my job? The nice new car? No idea. But somewhere in the back of my mind, I think perhaps not.

'Oh look, over there ...'

Negative thoughts will still pop up here and there. Sometimes you'll catch them, sometimes you won't. But as you move through the steps you will improve your general mood and, for the most part, be able to catch negative imaginings and not go for that ride down Pain Highway. When a doubtful thought enters your mind, instead of entertaining it and letting it grow you can hum softly and replace it with a little silent singing.

Or if singing isn't your thing, give your mind a problem to solve. Start to make a mental shopping list, trying to make yourself remember everything you need from the supermarket without writing it down. Ask questions: 'What do I want for dinner? What ingredients do I need for that? I think I've got enough salad but I'll need to get fresh coriander.'

You can even have a few mantras or affirmations on hand to change the direction of your thoughts. 'True love is for me' gets right to the point, and repeating it in your mind immediately interrupts the flow of thoughts. If this phrase does nothing for you, come up with something strong and personally meaningful to you. Distraction, preoccupation, whatever works for you. It sounds simple because it is. It literally takes a few seconds and it sends your mind in a different direction. Because if you want to live the life you say you do, at the risk of boring you to tears from repetition, you need to change your focus.

Stop scaring yourself thinking about what you don't want, what hurt you and what didn't work out. You have to let that stuff go and start thinking more about what you do want or about things that are completely neutral emotionally. You've done the work to disengage those neural pathways that associate love with pain and disappointment; don't let them start firing up again. You need to protect the investment you've made in yourself and make the decision to look for things that make you happy and feel good. It's a small decision that can net big results. But if you do 'go for the ride' and negative thoughts get the better of you, don't compound things by beating yourself up for your inability to divert yourself with more pleasant topics. Let it run its course then, when it has exhausted itself, get back to feeling good. Don't think about it or give it more attention or energy. Let it go and get on with your day.

Letting go

We've talked about keeping your mind focused on what you want while expecting your person to arrive, but we haven't really talked about faith. It's a big word, a big concept and maintaining it isn't always easy when you're sitting in the waiting room of love. It requires a certain amount of composure and an understanding of the way things work at this stage of the game. And it all centres around balance.

The balance you need this far down the unsingling path is between action and letting go. At first it sounds like a contradiction. Action implies intent. You take action because you want a certain result, the desired result here being meeting the love of your life. Letting go on the other hand means releasing, relaxing and, some would say, inaction. Therefore letting go seems to be action's opposite. It isn't.

At some point in unsingling you have to trust: trust that the momentum, the love and the good vibes you've been putting out will come to fruition. You can and should still use your steps while allowing things to unfold. So how do you do that? By believing everything is in order, and that your true love will come to you at exactly the right time in the perfect place. This belief helps you to let go.

An inside job

Faith is often defined as the absence of doubt. Another more realistic definition would be that faith is the ability to move beyond your doubts, remaining focused on what you want and returning to it after any trust wobbles. That's my definition anyway. Achieving this helps build faith in yourself because when you can stand back and acknowledge that you have moved past your doubts (and any unpleasant memories) and kept right on believing in love, you develop confidence in *you*. And that confidence will make your life easier. Not just when it comes to romance, but in every area of your life.

Unsingling is about finding your true love, that's for certain. It's also about turning to yourself to find what you need, reclaiming the emotional self-sufficiency that may have been trained out of you over the years. Think about it. Have any of the steps asked you to do anything outside yourself apart from those few initial creative projects and clearing your living space? Unsingling is an internal job, designed to flip the switch in your mind that has been keeping you from your dearest wish. Your emotions, thoughts and feelings have great power and you've been learning to harness and direct that power to achieve what you want, using all the tools you have at your disposal to renew your belief in love.

You've started to take notice of how you feel and where your thoughts and emotions are at. And wherever possible, moving them in the direction you want them to head. And when you can manage that, you're in charge and you won't be left wanting. Giving you the job of keeping yourself balanced and happy makes sense. Yes, other people – your true love in particular – will support you whenever and wherever they can. But being able to keep yourself on an even keel more of the time will make life more enjoyable and you a lot happier. And it will help the relationship that's coming to you stay strong.

You've come a long way, baby. Don't stop now, because things are about to get even better.

Minding the gap checklist

♥ Singing, humming and dancing are all good ways to set your mood for the day, particularly if you tend towards seriousness or often worry. Also, having an upbeat song you love in reserve to hum or sing softly to yourself when your mind's wandering into dubious territory can be a good distraction. It can set your thoughts in a different direction, getting you back on course and saving you the trip down Pain Highway.

♥ If your mind refuses to be deflected and insists on thinking about bad times, don't compound it by beating yourself up for your inability to divert yourself with more pleasant topics. Let it run its course then, when it has exhausted itself, get back to feeling good. Don't think about it or give it more attention or energy. Let it go and get on with your day.

♥ Laugh whenever and wherever you can. Overwrought intensity isn't going to bring your lovely fellow to you any faster. Remember to breathe.

♥ Having faith refers to achieving an important balance. It's about stoking the sense of anticipation, and keeping you focused on what you want, to stop you thinking about what you don't. And it's also about letting go. At first this sounds like a contradiction, but you'll discover as you go forward with your unsingling that it feels exactly right. Because holding on too tight squeezes all the joy and fun out of your experience. And when you enjoy the whole process, you'll be happy and confident when your true love turns up.

♥ The old saying 'A watched pot never boils' applies here. You need to find the ability within yourself to remain focused, continuing your steps while allowing things to unfold in your life. This means letting go and trusting.

♥ Faith is defined as the absence of doubt. Another more realistic definition could be the ability to move beyond your doubts, keeping focused on what you want and returning to it after any trust wobbles. This process will help build faith in yourself, because knowing there is a part of you that's strong enough to move beyond those doubts is big. It helps you believe in yourself, and acknowledging your achievement increases self-confidence.

♥ Giving yourself the job of staying balanced and happy makes sense. Other people will support you whenever and wherever they can, but being able to keep yourself on an even keel most of the time will make life more enjoyable and you'll be a lot happier. And it will help the relationship that's coming to you stay strong.

Step 7
False starts

Patience is the art of concealing your impatience.
— Guy Kawasaki

This is an interesting time for you. You've probably been doing your practices for some time now and you can feel the momentum building. You want to remain relaxed and calm but there is an element of excitement that has you aware of what is going on around you. Very aware. As much as you'd like to say you're super-cool and one hundred per cent trusting that your fabulous fellow is going to turn up at exactly the right time, somewhere in the back reaches of your mind there's a level of concern: What if you miss him? What if he misses you? Part of you knows that the old saying 'What is meant for you can't go past you' is true. But part of you, the part that has a little trouble trusting in life, is worried that you might be looking the other way when he turns up.

You picture it like the classic movie scene where the lovers continue to just miss each other. One gets out of the cab and strides away while the other gets in the other side. One walks in the front door just as the other exits the back. One finally decides to call while the other struggles to answer, balancing the shopping and their keys, dropping their phone down the grate. You've seen it a hundred times. A bit frustrating admittedly, but you don't worry because you know it will all turn out well in the end. And it will. We talked about faith in the last chapter and you need to exercise a little faith here. Yes, someone to love is coming into your life. No, you don't know what he looks like, what he does for a living or how you'll recognise him. But you will feel a certain way when you're around him, more yourself – your real self. Maybe not immediately, but you will know. You will not be looking in the wrong direction and you won't miss him, so relax.

Let's go back to the example of the person waiting for someone to join them in a café. Is she sitting on the edge of her seat, desperately scanning every face that walks into the café, eyes wet, wide and afraid until her friend shows up? Hopefully not. She'd put people off their skinny lattés. Most likely she's reading a magazine or playing with her phone, drinking her coffee and enjoying herself until her person arrives. She'll glance up occasionally, probably do a quick scan of the crowd but she knows they'll turn up. She's not concerned. This is the way you need to approach meeting the love of your life. Give yourself this opportunity to be quietly confident. Haven't you always wanted to be one of those poised, cool and ever-so-slightly reserved women? This is your chance. *Allow* good things to come to you. Trust that they will. And if you have to breathe into a paper bag occasionally, do that too. Just make sure you get back to trusting as soon as you're done. Let Team Love do its fine work in your life and let go.

Do what you feel led to do

This is not to say that if your instincts tell you to join a certain gym, class or dating site you should ignore them. Please don't. What I'm saying is: follow your internal promptings. But don't get yourself into a state worrying that you'll overlook him somehow, believing frenzied activity or proactive searching will bring him to you more quickly. It won't. In fact, dating a lot of different people might just confuse matters.

Unsingling is a mixture of art and science. The art is the creative practice you've used to support the science, retraining your neural pathways to align with true love, the kind that lasts forever. These processes have changed your predominant thoughts and feelings about love to something infinitely more positive. Unsingling is about doing everything you can and then handing it over to love, knowing you *will* be in the right place at the right time. Trusting that when you meet your lovely man it will be easy and natural, you'll start to talk and everything will flow from there.

You've changed your beliefs about yourself and about love and made it accessible, comfortable, warm, safe and ordinary. Normal. It's no longer this mystical faraway land you'll never get to. It's right there next to you. You own it. It's yours. And even if you're insides are jittering, play a game with yourself. You've imagined yourself happy, secure, already in a great relationship. You've used your imagination to experience what it feels like to flip the switch and be a person who has someone loving you in exactly the way you've always wanted to be loved. Use your imagination to see yourself as that woman in the café, totally at ease in your own skin, knowing your love will show up and you won't miss him. Let yourself unwind a little, enjoy your latté and stop jumping out of your skin at every man who says hello. You're making yourself – and everyone around you – nervous.

Having said all that you will be putting out some pretty powerful vibes and you might find yourself the object of interest because of the energy you're exuding. You will most likely notice an increase in attention from the opposite sex, often subtle but nevertheless there. Even people who've known you for years might be looking more closely as if trying to work out what's different about you. You probably haven't changed your hair, lost or gained much weight, or bought significantly different clothes. The allure of a woman who feels good about herself and about life is a powerful thing. These processes will likely have caused a shift in you. There will be an extra vibration in the air around you; that indefinable something that other people will pick up on, and men will respond to. You might even get asked out on dates, and have to negotiate the intricacies of whether to go or opt out. And this can be tricky.

The thunderbolt and the slow burner

What I'm going to say now will be repeated a few times because it's important. Just because you are in the process of unsingling yourself does not mean the first man that shows an interest in you is the One. The sort of thinking you need to avoid is this: 'I've been visualising and imagining true love coming into my life, so whoever comes along first has to be my person.' Not necessarily.

Unsingling has a specific focus and it's not about taking whatever's on offer. It is about true love, the kind that stands the test of time and lasts forever. That's the goal. And that being the case, discernment needs to be employed. At the other end of the spectrum you also don't want to assume that true love has only one way of coming into your life, i.e. the thunderbolt. The type of thinking that insists 'The moment we meet, angels will sing, skyrockets will take flight and a shaft of light will stream from above and shine on us both.' I'm exaggerating to make a point, but you get the gist. In 'Step 2: Finding treasure' I said that being adamant your fellow looks a certain way, enjoys certain hobbies or works in a particular job can block true love from coming to you. You don't want to be restricting yourself by putting conditions on *how* this person comes into your life. The way he comes into your life is up to life. And love. All you need to take note of is how you *feel* when you are around him.

The thunderbolt *may* come and knock you for a six, angelic choirs may serenade you, and heavenly light may illuminate you both; and if this happens, that's wonderful. But it doesn't always happen that way. True love can come along in ways that take a little longer to recognise but are equally valid. If you feel you can be yourself when you are in his company that is a very good start. Your true love story might start in a very low key manner. It could be a lovely slow burner. From small beginnings big things can grow.

Slow burners don't include men who ask you out and in whom you have absolutely no interest, because that's straightforward. Your internal answer is immediate and definite. Some people, for whatever reason, will never touch your heart. What we're going to concentrate on here is making sure you don't backtrack into accepting anything less than what feels special to you. It's time to acknowledge your inner genius, your expert status when it comes to you and your heart.

Now you know there's something infinitely preferable waiting for you. Not perfect, but warm and safe and full of love. So it's time to be scrupulously honest with yourself, which means, when you meet someone *don't superimpose the feelings you want to be experiencing over the top of your actual feelings*. You might be tempted to do this in your determination to make this relationship happen *now*. That sort of impatience is risky. It can lead you away from the good that love has in store for you.

Trust your feelings

People have long been known to rush into relationships because they're so eager to be swept away they haven't taken a realistic look at the person they are handing their heart to. But that time is past. Yes, he might have gorgeous eyes and great shoulders but did you really think it was okay that he checked his phone while you were telling him about your weekend or about some difficult situation at work you needed help with? Or did a little alarm bell go off in your head? If it did, you may have wandered into false start territory.

Unfortunately, false starts aren't always immediately recognisable but there are often warning signs. That's why it's important to remain aware of your true feelings and reactions when you're with someone new. No-one, not even your soul mate, is perfect. Even with the greatest love there may be moments when you feel a slight 'disconnect', when they say or do something that surprises you and you're not sure you sync with it. Thankfully, with the right person those moments are relatively rare. You certainly don't want to run screaming at the first sign of any slight discord.

But if there's a new person in your life whom you're considering for the position of the One, but he often makes you uneasy or uncomfortable, you need to take note of what your feelings are telling you. This is not the time to put your hands over your ears and sing 'la la la la' in an attempt to outrun your disquiet. It's time to stand still and acknowledge what is. Because when you take your attention away from trying to force something to happen and simply observe, allowing things to unfold, your feelings will tell you everything you need to know. Focus on how you *feel* and if it isn't an absolutely unequivocal yes then it's a 'maybe', and 'maybe' means keeping your heart safe in your own keeping for the moment. If it's a 'no' you need to honour that. And you can offset any disappointment with the reassuring knowledge that those icky feelings you've been experiencing and trying to ignore won't be making an appearance in your true love show. They don't feature on the program.

An easy way to differentiate any potential suitors and help you sort the wheat from the chaff is to tune in to your body and your senses. When your true love appears your feelings will centre on your heart; it will feel fuller. If it's a false start the majority of sensation will centre in your gut. There will probably still be some plummeting excitement and squirmy feelings in your tummy with your true love too because, let's face it, meeting the love of your life is exciting stuff. But there will be a discernible warmth in your heart as well. False starts make your stomach squirm, but not in such a nice way. You might also find yourself knocking into furniture, dropping things, tripping, even falling over – all little warning signs from your intuitive self that you're heading in the wrong direction and are ignoring your instincts that this fellow is not for you.

For those of you who've convinced yourself you're not a feeler, that you're more cerebral and your heart and stomach are just organs to pump blood around your body and digest food, you will most likely want to think your way through whether a person is right for you. Write the old pros and cons list. That's the way your feelings express themselves, through intellectual activity. And it's a great way to clarify things when you're confused. Sometimes the simple act of getting things out of your head and onto a piece of paper helps enormously. You can see, in black and white, if you're just being a bit picky or if your concerns are well founded. If you're still confused at the end of compiling your list, it means the answer isn't apparent yet and you'll just have to wait and see.

Give me a sign

Just as your inner world can give you signs, so can the world around you if you remain aware. As in movies where the character begs for some direction, looking to heaven for an answer, the world can give you signals if you are open to them.

I know of someone who was going out on a third date with a man she so wanted to be the One, despite her misgivings about him and their compatibility. Trying to ignore her doubts, on the way to meeting him she drove past a building site plastered with the same billboard advertising the name of a play for an entire city block. The billboard said three words: 'The Wrong Man'. An entire block of posters shouting 'The Wrong Man'. To make things worse the traffic lights stopped her there so she had to sit *absorbing* the message for several minutes with no escape. Feeling like she'd been given a very clear sign, she could no longer ignore the truth and ended their budding relationship that day.

Less than a year later she met another man – the right man – and they've been very happily together ever since.

Whether you're a 'thinker' or a 'feeler' if you've met someone and for any reason you have a serious question mark above your head – when you are with him, when you think about him or when you have returned from a date – acknowledge and honour that hesitation. In the past you might have beaten any doubts into submission, determined this person was going to be the One, shoving that very square peg into that rounder-than-round hole and declaring it a perfect fit. But you know better now. You're expecting the real deal and you're prepared to wait if you have to, which is a very nice, very empowering place to be. You're ready.

Going with your gut

In case there are some of you who still feel slightly dubious about your aptitude for sorting the 'good 'uns' from the 'not suitables', or if you need a little more clarity about how to deal with potential suitors in an appropriate unsingling fashion, let's imagine a situation that will help illustrate what we've been talking about.

You have a cute new work colleague who starts to pay you a lot of attention. He's attractive and funny and of course you wonder if this could be Him. You're sort of interested, but something – and you can't say exactly what – is telling you to watch and wait. When you ask yourself how you feel about him it's a maybe, which takes you a little by surprise. Before you started your unsingling you would have been thrilled to have someone like him take such an interest. You feel a little let down that this won't be the thunderbolt or love at first sight you'd been hoping for. But, proud and relieved, you're behaving like an adult and not plunging from the high board without first dipping your toe in the water, maybe for the first time in your life. That, and you don't fancy having to look for a new job if it all turns pear-shaped.

About a week after he began seeking you out, he asks you to dinner. You make an excuse then immediately regret it. You start to wonder why you're hesitating. He's attentive, says all the right things, so you resolve to try to engineer another invitation to which you'll say yes. When you get home you spend the entire night kicking yourself for being so reticent and get up early the next day to make yourself look extra special for work. You enter the office in your best outfit, ready to casually mention you're free that evening. Fortuitously enough he's in the kitchen, talking to someone, when you go to make yourself coffee. But before you can say anything he makes a comment about his ex to his companion you find so offensive that, before he's even finished his sentence, you taste the bitter tang of disappointment, quickly followed by a tsunami of relief that you heeded your feelings.

Maybe he was annoyed you'd refused his offer the day before and said it to goad you. Maybe he didn't. It doesn't really matter. Whatever his intention, he gave you a glimpse of the inner workings of his mind and this man is definitely not for you. And because of your respect for yourself and your new-found ability to not try to please everybody all the time you said no and saved yourself the messiness of extricating yourself from a romance that was doomed from the start. Your feelings were spot on and knowing this gives you confidence in them. And in yourself. It may not have been the outcome you were hoping for, but it's still a brilliant result. Sometimes you only realise you've changed when you're challenged. Well done you.

Take care, take your time, trust yourself

If you're feeling anything like one would hope at this advanced stage of unsingling, you're not in the mood to waste time with a relationship that is going nowhere. You're ready for the love of your life and anything else is a distraction you simply don't need or, worse, might damage your renewed belief in love. And you've come way too far to risk that.

Cautiousness has had a bad rap over the years when it comes to relationships. Being wary or even simply taking your time to see *how* you feel about a person means, some would say, that you lack spontaneity, passion, fire. To be truly living you need to throw restraint to the wind and just go for it. Not in unsingling. Caution is the new cool, as seen in the previous example. Having to look for a new job because an office romance went south isn't what you want to be thinking about right now. If it's true love, it's not going anywhere.

If you have any reservations about a potential partner, keep in mind that organisational psychologists recommend interviewing a job applicant on three separate occasions on three different days in three different venues, as studies suggest this will help you discover who someone really is all the way down, not just their surface persona. Consider getting together with a new man a few times in a few different settings before making any commitment, suss him out a little bit (but don't bring out the psychometric test papers – that might be going too far!).

So take your time if that feels like the right thing to do. But just because you're exercising a little caution does not mean you can't go out with someone if it *feels* right. Workplace scenarios like the one above need to be treated carefully, however if someone from the office asks you out, and he seems nice enough and you sense a warmth there, you might decide that you'd like to get to know him better. Make a date for something easy, like meeting for a late breakfast on the beach in a casual café and see what happens. Of course, in the back of your mind you'll be wondering if he'll turn out to be important, but the truth is you don't know yet. Wait and see. It's okay to not know what you think about someone at first. Chances are you will feel there's something slightly special about him if he is your true love, and the more time you spend with him the warmer your feelings will become. This is classic slow burner stuff – a lovely, gradual realisation that this person is the one for you. And if in the past you've thought every man you ever dated was special and your destiny, relax. Do things differently this time. The answer will come.

Everyone tries to put on a good front when they've met someone they like, to put their best self forward. It's a well-known and accepted part of courtship. Spending a little time getting to know someone can help you avoid starting something you're just going to have to finish if the two of you turn out to be a bad fit. Theoretically speaking, somewhere with a very relaxed atmosphere and daytime dates like the one mentioned above make the most sense if you want to check someone out a little and get to know them better until you're sure.

Alcohol is definitely a relaxant, but depending on the effect it has on you, you might want to make the first date an alcohol-free zone. If you decide to go to a bar or restaurant you might want to limit yourself to one or two drinks. Overindulging isn't always conducive to being your best self, so try to ensure the setting is geared towards having fun rather than you feeling embarrassed afterward. Then again, true love might come in the guise of dinner, dancing and champagne; this might be just as fitting as a leisurely brunch and a stroll on the beach.

Keep trusting yourself and listening to what your insides are telling you and you can't go wrong. You might have the worst date in the world but something deep in your heart tells you to persist, that this person could be the one for you. True love doesn't always start in the smoothest, most elegant way. Or you might have the most perfect date ever conceived, the guy doing everything just right, but you know deep down he isn't the One. It's a mysterious thing.

Your true love story could start in a myriad of ways. It could be a lovely gradual realisation that this person is the one for you, and the more time you spend together the more certain you are that he is the One. It could even turn out to be someone you've known for years, but because of the fine work you've been doing transforming your beliefs about love you suddenly see this person with new eyes, as he does you, and your love story starts that way. Or you might experience the thunderbolt, with cupid's arrow simultaneously piercing your hearts. Whatever way it arrives in your life, love coming to town is something to celebrate. When you know, you know.

Enjoy!

False starts checklist

♥   You've changed. Trust that the changes in your psyche will manifest in your experience. You now know that love is right there for you. It's normal, everyday, extraordinary in its ordinariness. It's nothing to be frightened of and everything to be excited about. You own it. It's yours, and it's the next obvious step. Relax.

♥   Trust your instincts. If they are telling you to join a certain club, dating site or enrol in a particular class heed them. But if something inside is telling you to just take it easy and do what you normally do, stick with that. If any out-of-your-ordinary-routine action is required on your part, you will know. Until then, stay cool.

♥   If warning bells are going off about a potential love, heed them. If something's telling you to run, lace up your running shoes and get going. Unsingling isn't about taking what's on offer. It's about the One. Don't let your desire to be in a relationship override good sense.

♥   How you feel is everything and you are the only one who knows with absolute certainty how a person affects your emotions and your sense of self. If your friends or family proffer an opinion, listen to it but make up your own mind. If you feel genuinely good about yourself when you're with him, that's likely an indication that something special is afoot.

♥   At some point you have to just let go and trust. Trust yourself and this process and keep calm. What is meant for you won't go past you so relax and breathe. Remember to let air continue to circulate in your life.

Part 3

Your true love relationship

Step **8**
True love

Come live in my heart, and pay no rent.
— Samuel Lover

I still have my unsingle filter working for me even though I've been with my husband seven years. I still make the same choices that I did when I first decided to unsingle myself. I actively seek out examples of couples who are obviously in love. I watch them being interviewed, I read about them in magazines. I pass on great stories I've heard about a couple doing nice things for each other, to make everyone feel good. And for the most part, I still don't watch movies or programs where hearts are being broken unless I know they'll be fixed by the end. I continue to avoid articles about why couples broke up and who did what to whom. I'm not interested. I like hearing about and seeing couples having a great time together. That makes me happy. I'm also fond of seeing the old classic – people walking along holding hands. But I think my favourite is when I see a couple laughing together, their faces creased up in enjoyment. It never fails to make me feel all warm and fuzzy inside.

There's some inextricable link between love and happiness, I think. Just like the synergy between action and letting go I talked about in 'Step 6: Minding the gap'; they help strengthen each other. The whole is greater than the sum of its parts. In true love relationships, happiness usually comes with the territory.

It's part of the package deal. But there's nothing wrong with making an effort to amp it up every now and then, doing things that will make you and your partner smile.

Modern mythology

It might be timely to clear up a few common myths about true love. In fact, it would be a disservice to this type of love and to unsingling, not to address them. Because you can guarantee that the couples I've read about in the multitude of studies and surveys on lasting love, who still rate themselves as being madly in love after ten or more years together, have been through some stuff together. Life is still life, even though you've got someone amazing to share it with. The results of one study in particular stayed with me. Imagine after twenty years of marriage rating your spouse above even your best friend in the friendship stakes (see Appendix 2). These couples' love is as strong as ever, perhaps even stronger as a result of everything they've experienced; not despite everything they've been through, but because of it.

Myth number 1: you will no longer have any problems

True love is not an eraser that rids your life of all hardship. But it does make you substantially happier. Having someone by your side and facing your challenges together definitely helps. And working through any challenges you might face *within* your relationship can make you grow closer as a couple, if you handle them in the right way.

Myth number 2: you don't have to work at it

There are no two ways about it. You have to work at it. Relationships don't exist in a vacuum. While researching this book I read more than my fair share of studies conducted by neuroscientists on lasting love and the positive effects it has in just about every area of your life. One of the common denominators across all the surveyed couples who still rated as being 'madly in love' after over ten years together was that their relationship was amongst their highest priorities. They didn't figure it would look after itself because it was of such inherent quality. Quite the opposite. These couples knew they had found something precious and worthwhile, and *wanted* to make the effort to ensure it flourished and grew. When you love someone you want to do things for your partner that will make them smile or ease their day. It's your pleasure and your privilege.

Your relationship will be a constant in your life, something you can count on. And your commitment to one another and to maintaining that love is what will keep it strong.

Ever after

Keeping that in mind, before you climb onto your trusty steed and head off on your true love adventure let's have a look at a few of the more obvious issues and behaviours couples need to navigate as they share their lives together. They include:

- **economy of grumbling**
- **differences of opinion**
- **a generous spirit**
- **just being silly**
- **where the romance is.**

Remember the unsingling tools you've used along the way? Keep them handy and let's see if we can utilise some of them to help guide you through.

Economy of grumbling

It's pretty safe to assume that when sharing a life with someone some things will crop up that annoy you about your true love, and vice versa. It's also safe to assume you've learnt enough through the unsingling process that you're going to handle these annoyances in a way that preserves the great love you've found. What I will say is this: from my observation true love relationships seem to let more things slide than most – it's the relationship equivalent of 'don't sweat the small stuff'. And really, when you think about it, this makes perfect sense.

You wanted a loving relationship so you put in the work to change your ideas about love to beliefs that did it justice. You stopped thinking about what disappointed you, what hurt and what didn't work out. You let that old neural net die and started to think about how fab love is, how much fun it is and how good being loved feels. Now that you've found your person, does it really make sense to throw all that out, to slide backwards into focusing on little things that bug you about each other so your vision is clouded and your joy diminished? Of course it doesn't. The thirteenth-century Persian poet Rumi said, 'Out beyond ideas of right and wrong, there is a field. I'll meet you there.' I think Rumi was an unsingler. Right and wrong are subjective; happiness is universal. Keep focusing on happiness, keep those positive neural pathways humming and happiness will continue choosing you.

A helpful hint: one of the surprising things that being in a true love relationship has taught me is that spending time together when you are annoyed with each other can actually help. I'd always thought taking time out was the best solution when you were irritated with your partner. But what I've found is sometimes grievances fade away if you simply sit near one another, hold each other's hand and enjoy your love's touch. Your breathing syncs, you both calm down and love smooths the ruffled feathers or sharp edges. Try it. Sitting close to each other on the couch, watching something that makes you both laugh is not the worst way to forget any niggles either of you might have. For some people it's better to change the venue; maybe taking a walk together to get ice cream. Or perhaps the beach is your happy place. Some fresh air and a stroll on the sand holding hands might help you both calm down. Try a few different things and you'll find what works for you.

Remember the cumulative effect we talked about in 'What you look for is what you'll find' and 'The yay! experiment', how focusing on finding the good in something or someone brings more of the same to you? Economy of grumbling is based on the same premise. This isn't a new concept for you. Keep focusing on the good and your life together will be warm and full of love. Not perfect, but happy. And isn't that what we all want?

Differences of opinion

As with economy of grumbling, it's pretty safe to assume there will be times when you and your true love see things differently. So what do you do when you can't agree to disagree, and things are getting a little hot under the collar – and not in a good way?

One of the most incisive things I've ever read about a couple handling themselves when they were heading down this road was recounted in *Committed*, Elizabeth Gilbert's sequel to *Eat, Pray, Love*. She and her Brazilian partner Felipe were travelling the globe in a sort of exile, as his US visa had been denied. It was a difficult situation they were trying to make the most of while their lawyer sorted the problem out, but they were getting on each other's nerves, as couples sometimes do, particularly in times of stress. When an argument threatened to blow out of control between the two of them, sitting on a hot, airless bus as they bumped their way through Asia, Felipe said, 'We need to be careful here'. He was referring to the fact that they'd both been through nasty divorces and knew that some things once said can never be taken back. If there were a Nobel Peace prize for relationships, he'd get my vote for that simple sentence.

Any conflict resolution expert will tell you the way you phrase your argument is paramount. You can say exactly the same thing, but in a way which will have your partner wanting to work with you. Don't prolong or exacerbate the argument so that one or both of you say things that are really hurtful or, in the most extreme case, beyond forgiveness. My suggestion is to avoid anything along the lines of 'If we can't sort this out, I think we should break up'. It's too confrontational and it's likely you don't actually mean it. The focus will be on the red-flag words in the second part of the sentence – 'break up' – and the issue at hand will probably be overlooked and remain unresolved.

Threats usually mean everything is brought up and the reason the argument began is forgotten. So by the end you're angry about things that weren't even on the table in the first place. It's counterproductive. A statement like 'I love you and want us to be happy, so I think we need to sort this out' is strong and straightforward. Your point is made in a way that will have the two of you working together for a common goal – sorting things out and remaining happily coupled. And this sort of direct phrasing means you'll be more likely to address the actual issue. The choice is between throwing kerosene or water on the fire. Not many of us enjoy arguing with someone we love, and in true love relationships this is particularly so. But you will find, as time goes by and you've been through your share of 'stuff' together, you've learnt more about each other. You begin to know the things each of you is sensitive about, and you understand each other at a deeper level. You learn not to ruffle each other's feathers and hurt each other's feelings and you become even closer. Having someone who knows you all the way through is a pretty special feeling. And getting to that point usually means you've been through your challenges as a couple and worked together to sort them out. The bond between you becomes even stronger. The love you share continues to grow.

A *generous* spirit

Imagine you come home from work, you've had a tough day and you feel done in. Even seeing your true love doesn't really make you smile. Instead of taking offence at your lacklustre greeting, he recognises that you're stressed and offers to run you a bath and light some candles. He even asks what sort of essential oil you'd like. His entire focus is on making you feel better. Before you know it you're sinking into the warm, fragrant water and your muscles release their death grip on your shoulders. You begin to feel human again. When you get out of the bath you're ready to have a nice night instead of feeling stretched thin. You give him the world's biggest hug and marvel at how much difference a small, loving gesture makes. You feel blessed.

This is the sort of behaviour that works for everyone. Long-term happy couples nurture each other and do kind things for one another as a matter of course. If your love comes home from work needing to talk, you listen and you're there for him. If he's the one that's had the hard day, you order take-out from his favourite restaurant or give him a back rub or whatever you think will make him feel better. You make an effort for each other. One of the things I like best about true love is its generous spirit and its reciprocity. It's not nit-picky or mean, and it doesn't keep score. It has a very big heart.

Looking after one another, going out of your way for each other and seeking the best in your true love comes naturally because true love relationships are reciprocal by nature. There's no danger you'll be the one making all the effort while your partner laps it up and gives nothing in return. You give a little extra here; they give a little extra there. When you're with the right person it all balances out somehow and you both benefit. Everybody wins.

The survey of marital generosity

An American study, The National Marriage Project, compiled data from three studies, the smallest of which involved 1630 married couples and was entitled 'The survey of marital generosity'. Project director Bradford Wilcox, with colleague Jeffrey Dew, wrote a working paper on the project called 'Give and you shall receive? Generosity, sacrifice and marital quality', which said their research supported the premise that acts of generosity are strong contributors to a healthy marriage. (This study concentrates on married couples but I believe the findings are applicable to all true love, committed relationships.)

Their paper said the survey's data showed that acts of generosity between a husband and wife, including small acts of kindness like making each other a coffee in the morning, treating each other with respect, regular displays of affection and being willing to forgive their spouse's faults was causally linked to marital satisfaction, and substantially decreased the likelihood of marital conflict or divorce. Their overall findings were that regular expressions of everyday generosity amongst couples (aged 18–55) were linked to higher quality contemporary marriages.

See? It's true. Everybody wins.

Just being silly

One of the loveliest things about having someone to share your life with is you can let your true self shine. Not the shiny, polished society you, the *you* you are when the front door is shut and you are home for the night. Remember in 'Step 6:

Minding the gap' you got the opportunity to lighten up and sing into your hairbrush, even if it was only in the privacy of your bathroom? You rediscovered how much fun it is to be silly. *Now you have someone to play with.* You can delight in the fact that you get to see a side of each other that your work colleagues (and most definitely your bosses) would never believe existed. You have an excuse to allow the childish, and sometimes perfectly infantile, part of yourself to re-emerge. Take advantage of it.

Look for opportunities to be silly. Have competitions about stupid things. Chase him around the house as a prank. Sing him little songs on his voicemail so he'll have something to make him smile when he can get to his phone. He'll probably do the same for you. Ask him to do a victory dance for you when his team scores a goal. When his knee starts going and his fist starts pumping the air you'll probably find yourself giggling uncontrollably, adding to the general hilarity of the man-dance. If you're partner's a really good dancer, maybe ask him to lose the smooth moves and channel his father getting on down for your amusement. If his father's a cool dancer too I'm afraid you're out of luck, but you get my drift. Let your inner kid come out to play.

One of my favourite stories about at-home silliness was something I heard a while ago, and thinking about it still makes me smile. A very funny young British actress was a guest on *The Ellen DeGeneres Show* and was talking about her husband's penchant for doing spontaneous, hands-on-hip lunges around the house which, seeing as he is long and lanky, would be particularly hilarious. Apparently the two of them often have a boogie when they are home alone, just for a laugh. As she spoke she seemed genuinely and effervescently happy, the sort of happiness that is catching. Watching her, I immediately resolved to incorporate lunging into our at-home dancing routine. It didn't last, of course; I think I pulled something. My husband was smart enough to not even attempt it. But it definitely made us laugh.

New true love is a great time to have some fun. And to be honest, you probably won't have to expend a lot of effort on keeping those neural pathways aligned with the happy and the light now that you've found your person. Happiness, as we've already discussed, tends to come with the true love territory. But there's nothing wrong with making an effort to amp it up every now and then, in true unsingling style. There's no such thing as too much happiness; so see how high yours can go.

Where the romance is

Romance, like happiness, is generally an inherent part of the true love experience. It's part of the package deal. And it isn't only found in large-scale, perfectly orchestrated events. Some of the world's most romantic gestures can be very small. Leave the television off for the night and turn on the music instead, sit and chat over a bottle of wine and a simple meal with candles, allowing yourselves to shift into a different gear. Find out new and amazing things about each other or ask your partner to retell stories you've heard before and loved. Ah, the lost art of conversation. It can be quite sexy. You might even feel like putting on your favourite smooching song and invite your love to do a slow dance around the lounge room. It's so nice when you take the time to connect, shutting out the outside world to be present in the moment.

Seeing Shakespeare in the Park on Valentine's Day is pretty romantic. Leaning into one another, lying on a blanket eating cheese and sipping champagne while *A Midsummer Night's*

Dream plays out around you is something you'll probably remember for quite a while.

Try reserving one night every week just for the two of you, when everyone knows you're not available. Take turns to buy great food and have a sort of lounge room picnic where no cooking is required. Take a breath, watch something together and enjoy each other's company with no distractions.

There can be great comfort and a certain amount of romance in these rituals, because weeks can fly by and sometimes you realise you haven't spent a single evening together. That one night is a definite in a busy life and it can give you something to look forward to all week. If you're always out, you might want to stay in and have the at-home picnic we just talked about. If you're often in, you might like to dress up and go to your favourite restaurant and take pleasure in each other's company.

Everyday romance, like leaving notes for one another, buying special treats for each other and really listening to each other are all contributors to making an ordinary life extraordinary. Bigger gestures might sometimes be called for and they are often things you'll always remember. But love and romance also live in quiet places and small deeds, giving your life together texture and meaning, helping you enjoy every step along the way.

What works for you

As part of my research for this chapter I read a study about long-term love and how to maintain it. It said one of the secrets to sustaining romantic love over the years is to continue learning and doing new and exciting things together. I suppose this is part of not making the assumption that because you've found your true love, you can switch onto automatic pilot and make no effort. I must admit that as I was reading, a question mark was hovering above my head. I went out and told my husband about the study and its conclusions. We both started nodding and saying things like, 'Excellent', 'Good idea' and 'That sounds about right'. Then after a moment I asked, 'When was the last time we learnt anything new and exciting together?' Duplicate blank expressions. The truth was out there. We just didn't want to admit it. Then, into the silence, trying to sound positive I said, 'I suppose we could take a cooking class together or, you know, a dance class.' We both looked horrified, glancing at each other trying to gauge the other's reaction. My husband saw my expression and said, 'It's just not us, is it?' We brightened, as if emerging from a very short, very dark tunnel. 'No. It just isn't us.' We didn't have to go into it further as we were of the same mind. For other couples, not doing new and exciting things together might spell disaster. But for the moment we're happy just the way we are.

This just goes to prove that, at least in our case, theories are great but they don't always fit. Who knows what the two of you will find romantic? That's something you'll find out together. Somehow when you're with your true love, things just tend to flow. You focus on happiness, togetherness and looking after each other and off you go. Love has come to town and you've jumped on that train. And wherever it's going, you know you're going there together.

True love checklist

♥ Your unsingle filter will continue working for you once you've found your true love, if you choose. You'll probably find what you're drawn to and what you bypass will remain the same, and you give your attention to things you like thinking about and observing. You continue to be a card-carrying member of Team Love.

♥ True love doesn't eliminate every problem from your life but it does make you substantially happier. And working through things together, making an effort to maintain the great love you've found is all part and parcel of lasting love. You become closer, not despite the things you go through and the challenges you face *but because of them*.

♥ Knowing that you found your true love because you changed your ideas about love, and that what you look for is what you'll find, use your time and attention to focus on the great and the good about your life together and don't waste too much time focusing on what is not.

♥ If you do find yourselves seeing things differently, try to use the least inflammatory language possible to resolve the issue. Take a deep breath and make sure the words you use focus on working things out and coming up with a solution. Arguments aren't necessarily what you'd choose, but they can help you get to know one another better. And the knowledge you glean from any upsets can help you avoid arguments in the future. You end up knowing and trusting your true love more than you thought possible, and your life together just keeps getting better and better.

♥ True love relationships have a generous spirit and are reciprocal by nature. You look after and take care of each other because you want to. In a busy world, that sort of love and attention is priceless.

♥ Now that you have someone to play with, take advantage of it. There's no safe limit to happiness so see how high yours can go. Let your inner kid re-emerge. Let yourself be silly.

♥ Romance can be found in unexpected places. Simply spending time together can be incredibly romantic, with all distractions switched off. Keeping one night a week that's reserved for the two of you can be a good idea if you're often both busy. Stay in or go out; find what works for the two of you.

♥ If you've read about an activity or behaviour that is recommended to keep romance alive but makes both of you want to run away or laugh, it probably isn't for you! Theories are great and can be a useful source of information, but if a particular theory doesn't resonate with the two of you, you can safely assume it's okay to bypass it. Final authority always remains with you.

Step 9
Socialising unsingle style

The better part of valour is discretion.
— William Shakespeare

Once you've met your true love you'll be on cloud nine. It's so much fun to share your social life with your person, and outside the two of you there's also a big, wide world to enjoy. When you're an 'us' there'll be adjustments to integrate your new relationship status into the rest of your life. So let's make sure the unsingling vibe is carried through to all the socialising you're going to be enjoying now.

Having someone to play with and come with you to events, and finally being able to use your 'plus one', is a very welcome change. Those Sunday morning brunches with your friends see you happily sharing your Big Breakfast with your love. There's something so appealing about having that person with you to laugh with and lean against and hold hands with under the table, knowing that when the group breaks off to do their own thing you have your own special someone right by your side. It's amazing and spectacular and wonderful. The world is a beautiful place.

The times you two spend together when you're out don't need a lot of discussion, because you're on the same wavelength and love seeing each other happy. Of course, socialising extends beyond the bounds of your relationship and attending events as a couple, so let's broaden our scope to encompass the world outside the two of you.

The big, wide world

Your social life might now include double dating, your own social networking buddies, and girlfriends that you spend time with on your own. Sometimes when you've gone through a major change there's a transition period when you find you're catching up with yourself. Your new beliefs and behaviours take a while to filter into the rest of your life. When you're with your partner it's easy, but when you're socialising solo you might feel a little strange. You're still the same person but you have changed. Lots of things have changed. For some, the transition will be seamless and easy. For others, it will take some adjusting when it comes to your other relationships and how you socialise now.

So what aspect of socialising are we going to be discussing here? We'll look at social media behaviour now that you're part of a couple, then we'll talk about some helpful hints for 'real life' socialising. I'm not recommending a veto on either, so don't get yourself in a twist on that score. Neither is this a Martha Stewart-type guide to etiquette. This is about integrating the new unsingled you into your existing friendships and life, in a way that you feel good about.

Sharing online

Part of socialising – which these days includes social media – is what you choose to share with others about your relationship once you're partnered up. In my opinion, discretion is key. Why is discretion so important? Because it's respectful and it's the way true love rolls. People in true love relationships – people who are still madly in love after years and years together – are people who respect what they have. Trust is a key ingredient to the whole true love deal, and using discretion is part of building and maintaining that trust. Discretion in your social interactions supports respect and trust in a relationship. Discretion takes on a different meaning when there is another person to consider and you've moved from 'I' to 'us'.

The overshare
We all know what an overshare is – too much information, whether intentional or not. An unintentional overshare can leave you feeling out of sorts and wishing you hadn't gone there. These feelings don't fit with the great and the good that your life and your relationship have in store for you. Being respectful of the love you've found makes good unsingled sense. This person is going to be with you for the long haul, whereas the people you're currently sharing with may not be. Unsinglers err on the side of the undershare.

To post or not to post …
Why is erring on the side of the undershare important? Because, while finding out about each other is one of the most exciting things about new true love, really getting to know someone

takes time, no matter how immediate or deep the connection. Sometimes when you get along so well with someone and feel you know them so intimately so quickly, you believe you know everything about them. One of the bonuses of discretion is that you don't get yourself into hot water because you've assumed your partner will be fine with something it turns out he's not so thrilled with. And vice versa. These are the sort of things that aren't always obvious. He may have laughed when you showed him the photo you took of him coming out of the bathroom in which he looks like a hobbit. But putting that photo on your Facebook page, thinking 'He'll think this is hilarious' can lead to you being taken aback, and on the back foot when it turns out he's really offended and asks you to remove it sharpish. Oops!

If you're not sure, get some guidelines happening. Ask him about his preferences and, while you're at it, you can let him know yours. Because even if you are super-excited about your fabulous fellow and want to tell the world every single thing about him, you have to consider that he may not be quite so keen to have his personal behaviour and life displayed for public consumption. Perhaps he thought the hobbit photo was funny because it was just between the two of you.

Or maybe the reverse is true – you like your privacy whereas he's more extroverted with what he will share. If this is the case you need to let him know. The easiest way to deal with this is to find out what level of information your love is comfortable with having put out there, and make sure he knows the same for you.

To post or not to post..... that is the question

In person

Now that you've met your true love and are in a relationship, chances are you'll experience a shift in your social life itself. You will spend time as a couple with other couples. Even your time 'with the girls' can change. The three social situations we'll look at are:

- **double dating**
- **out with the girls**
- **one on one.**

Double dating

Part of the new true love experience is socialising with other couples, and this is usually lots of fun. You get to catch up, laugh, relax and enjoy everybody's company. Occasionally, though, it might not be quite so comfortable. There might be some couples who have a different take on their relationship and on relationships in general to the two of you. Their *modus operandi* is to criticise each other and bicker and try to pull you into it.

This isn't to be confused with friends who are occasionally a little difficult to be around or who are just having an off night. Or a bit of friendly teasing when everyone's having a laugh, with whoever's being teased grinning and enjoying the attention.

What we're talking about is the sort of behaviour that has you and your partner shifting in your seats and looking for the exit. If that's the case, you might find you spend less time with them. Or better yet, they start to avoid you because you're no fun, aka 'you don't dive right in there with them'. Excellent result. The decision's been taken out of your hands.

Within reason: the extended mix

Remember we talked about making judgement calls in Step 5 regarding when and where it's appropriate to remove yourself from negative relationship input, ensuring you don't make a spectacle of yourself in the process? That basic premise applies here very nicely. Here's another quick questionnaire:

1. Your parents have been married for many years and have a well-developed habit of bickering and strongly disagreeing on a wide range of subjects. Whenever you're around, they always turn to you mid-disagreement and say, 'I'm right, aren't I (insert your name)?' Now that you have a partner he often gets called on for his opinion and support. It is beyond awkward. How do you respond? Do you:
a) Run screaming from the house, yelling, 'You're infecting my neural pathways and my relationship!', dragging your partner with you?
b) Smile and say, 'You know I don't take sides with this stuff. How's Susie/Ellen/Uncle Bert?'
2. You're out for a gorgeous dinner with your love and another couple. You haven't treated yourself for ages and you're excited to be in a nice restaurant and are looking forward to a great evening. The couple start sniping at each other and the night looks set to take a sharp nosedive. Do you:
a) Run screaming from the restaurant, yelling, 'You're infecting my neural pathways and my relationship!' dragging your partner with you?

b) Pretend you haven't noticed and start talking about something you know they're interested in?

Will this work every time? Maybe not. Sometimes people will let themselves be diverted for a minute then, like a terrier with something between their teeth, head straight back to the original topic. There's not much you can do about it if that's the case. You just have to try to have the best time you can.

Tip: If you find yourself in this situation don't think about it or talk about it afterwards. Discussing other people's behaviour and their relationship is focused attention; you're looking for a neural bypass on this one. Get back to feeling good and chat to your true love about happier things.

Out with the girls

Socialising with the girls might be slightly different now that you're one of the 'coupled up' ones. You've moved categories and the discussions you find yourself part of, or the questions you find yourself subjected to, may have changed.

Girls who love their guys

Hopefully you have a great, supportive group of friends who are thrilled you've found someone special, who really like your fella and don't tend to spend too much time talking about their menfolk when they're out. If they do they've only got good things to say about their significant others. They might occasionally mention that their partner has been annoying lately but for the most part they don't go there. Perfect. You're in good company. You'll be able to let your hair hang down, talk about girly makeover shows or your jobs or the state of the nation for hours uninterrupted.

The 'us against them-ers'

This group is always going to be trickier to navigate. Somewhere along the way they've decided to see love as something to complain about. They might be quite happy that way, and their partners might be out doing the same thing with *their* friends. This doesn't mean, however, that when you're in their company you have to immediately drop what you know to be true for you, no matter how much pressure is brought to bear. This pressure can be subtle, or about as subtle as a poke in the eye. The whole 'us against them' theme can get old really fast if you no longer think this way, or if you never did but don't quite have the courage to say so.

Luckily there's an unsingling tool that can help: The 'broken record'.

The broken record

Being protective of your relationship when you're around people who want to dish dirt is the smart unsingle approach. If they're indiscreet about their own relationship, you know they're unlikely to be concerned about keeping to themselves what you say about your partner. For whatever reason some people like to create waves and unless you and your true love are on a surfboard, waves are something you can do without.

Someone gave me this advice years ago when I asked her how to deal with people like this and I think it's brilliant: when you're around people who like to seek out problems and discord, and who make complaining about love their favourite pastime, use what she calls the 'broken record'. It's another tool to put in your unsingle belt to be brought out whenever necessary. It's brilliant because it ensures smooth sailing.

What's the 'broken record'? Whenever a tricky person asks you about your partner, or how things are going between the two of you, you say the same thing every time. You might mix up the response occasionally or change the phrasing slightly, but the message is always the same. 'He's great. Thanks for asking. Everything's good.' 'Hmmm, really busy at work. Yes, everything's good.' 'He prepared a spectacular meal the other night. He's a great cook. I know, so lucky.' 'Yes, lovely. Nothing to report. Everything's good.'

Even if he left the toilet seat up that morning and you've had your cranky pants on all day about it, this is something you need to keep to yourself. Blurting out some annoyance that will have passed by the time you get home is a retrograde move. People who like to stir things up have elephantine memories – they never forget – and it will probably be the first thing they mention the next time they see your love. Imagine your 'friend', with the delivery of an auctioneer yelling across the room as you enter, 'Here's the caveman that leaves the toilet seat up. Didn't your mother teach you any manners?', leaving you between a rock and a hard place, wishing the floor would swallow you up.

The subject matter in this example isn't serious but the fact that you've spoken of him in a negative way behind his back will register. No-one likes to feel as if their private behaviour is subject to public scrutiny. It's disloyal and it puts a chink in the trust the two of you share, and it simply isn't worth it. That's where the broken record comes in. One of the best things about this tool is you never get caught on the hop. No matter who you're with, where you are, how nervous you might be or how much pressure is brought to bear to get you to spill the beans or join in, you have your reply ready. You never have to be concerned you'll blurt out something that you don't mean just to appease the company you're in.

If the group demands something negative on your fellow, it might work to tell the truth. Something like: 'I love him. I think he's amazing. He's the best thing that ever happened to me and he feels the same way about me. I've got nothing bad to say about him. If that makes me Pollyanna, that's okay.' That should have their jaws swinging. In fact you might want to get out your phone to take a picture because their expressions could be a special moment. However, if your statement has about as much impact as a twig in a tornado and they keep persisting, running away might be a good idea.

One on one

Discretion doesn't mean never discussing your relationship in any real way. Girls are girls and sometimes you need to talk it out. Even the greatest love requires adjustments as you move forward. Having a trusted friend, a person to confide in or ask advice of, can be a positive, as long as they like your partner and want the two of you to remain together. You might even be lucky enough to have two great, trustworthy friends and together the three of you can really help to sort your questions out. However, this doesn't include discussing private subjects that you know are just between the two of you. No matter how good a friend you have, there is some information you never share. If your partner has told you something in complete confidence, you need to honour it. Trust is a beautiful thing in a relationship. Treasure it.

Wise friends can often help you see things from a different perspective and are worth their weight in gold. If they're also funny and make you lighten up and laugh, their net worth goes up again. You will find the longer you've been with your true love, the less often you'll have issues that need workshopping. You work things through together and grow even closer – one of the benefits of long-term love.

If you're in a one-on-one situation with an 'us against them-er', talk about anything but your relationship. If they insist on news about your true love, use the broken record. Every time.

That's all, folks

You are in for some pretty fab times with your friends and your true love and now you have tools to help you along the way. Integrating your new unsingled status into your current social circle is something that should bring a smile to your face.

You've also learnt how to steer clear of any murky waters with people who like to stir the pot, and keep your happy relationship just that. Trust, discretion and respect are second nature in true love relationships. They keep the waters clear and inviting and the people who like creating waves won't even manage a ripple on the surface. You never know – your happy face might even convince them to cross over and start playing for Team Love for a while.

Let the good times roll. Have fun socialising unsingle style.

Socialising unsingle style checklist

♥ Time to have some fun! Socialising with your partner and having someone to go to events with is one of the great things about true love coming to town. Having someone to lean into and laugh with at duty-bound work events makes a big difference. Dance the night away; you deserve it.

♥ Sometimes transitioning from 'I' to 'us' requires some adjustment. Your new beliefs and behaviours take time to filter into the rest of your life. Go easy on yourself and enjoy the changes. Honour any new feelings you might have and don't feel you have to be exactly the same as you were before. Change is part of life and your good friends will roll with it.

♥ What you choose to share with others about your relationship is important. Discretion is key. People in true love relationships – people who are still madly in love after years and years together – are people who respect what they have. Discretion in your social interactions supports respect and trust in a relationship. It's the way true love rolls.

♥ Finding a happy middle ground is worthwhile when it comes to your relationship and how you incorporate it into your existing social life. When you're not with your partner, what you say about him in his absence shows a lot about your character and the person you are. Respect never goes out of style.

♥ If you used to have an 'everything out there' social media policy but something about it no longer sits right, that is *fine*. Honour any hesitation you might feel when you go to post something and get some guidelines happening with your love. Get to know what level of 'sharing' you're both comfortable with. And don't assume that just because he's male he won't care if you post hideously ugly photos of him as a joke. Chances are if you wouldn't like it done to you, he won't think it's funny either.

♥ 'Within reason', discussed in Step 5, applies here. You still want a neural bypass on negative relationship input. In some social situations, however, you're going to have to grin and bear it. If you're with a couple who are sniping and arguing or criticising, don't talk about it with your true love on your way home. Talking about other people's behaviour is still focused attention. Chat about happier things with your love, keeping those love neurons humming.

♥ Socialising without your partner should still be lots of fun. If you have friends who have a different take on love, and who make a habit of talking negatively about their partner when they're with the girls, employ the 'broken record' approach. This means giving bland, standard answers to any queries about how the two of you are going. Rinse and repeat.

♥ Having a trusted confidante or a couple of good friends you can talk to if you ever get confused about how to approach something along your true love adventure is not a bad thing. They can also help make you laugh. Having a friend like this in addition to your true love means you're doubly blessed.

Step **10**

Home is where the heart is

There's no place like home.
— John Howard Payne

I still clearly remember the nervous excitement I felt on the day I 'officially' moved in with my then fiancé, now husband. We'd been going out for three or four months and I'd spent nearly every night at his place anyway, so I don't know why I was nervous. Perhaps it was because I was leaving my little place and knew in my heart I wouldn't be going back. As I unpacked my things the nervousness started to take over the excitement. My love, being pretty attuned to my moods, took one look at my face, kissed the back of my neck and left me to it, disappearing into the bathroom.

Five minutes later he called me in and I saw what he'd been doing. The bath was running; he'd arranged scented candles around the tub and the bubble bath was starting to gently foam. (I know. He's a keeper.) Feeling better, I went back to finish unpacking the last few things. When I returned to the bathroom I saw the biggest, most perfect heart had spontaneously formed from the bubbles in my absence. I'd had baths there before using the same bubble bath, but this had never happened. I went and got my camera and took a picture because I wanted to remember how perfect it was. I felt as if Team Love was giving me the thumbs up. Looking at it, something inside me relaxed and let go and my nerves settled. I was home.

Your own little world

Sooner or later moving in together is generally part of the true love experience. And whether your home is modest or lavish, it's where the two of you get to rest and hang out. It's the place you get to shut the door at the end of the day and take a breath: your own little world. And whether you believe in *feng shui* or not, there is enough evidence to suggest that a living space which reflects and generates positive energy will support you as a couple. This chapter is not a guide to *feng shui*, although it does reference it. This is about helping you create a space that will support your relationship and make you both feel good.

Transforming your living space can be as cheap or expensive as you want, but often using inexpensive fabrics, lighting, cushions, vases, artwork and plants arranged effectively can successfully renovate a living space. It may take a little longer than if you had an unlimited budget, but shopping for home 'things' is a nice thing to do as a couple. It bonds you, and starts your life together as an 'us'. Whether you move into his place or he moves into yours, or you find a new place together, you'll still both have your own 'stuff'. Some of this will have positive memories, some possibly negative, and some just won't suit you as a couple. You need to discuss what pieces you like and dislike, what makes you feel 'up' and what doesn't. You might not totally agree on everything and need to meet somewhere in the middle. Remember, you're on a new journey and your environment should reflect both of you.

So what are we talking about exactly? Here are some ways to help you create a harmonious home.

Clear, clean space

In Step 1 I talked about keeping the bedroom, particularly the bed, clear of clutter to invite love in. Now that love has come in and made itself at home you need to keep your bedroom clutter-free. Clutter in the bedroom is said to indicate, in *feng shui* terms at least, disorganisation and a lack of focus and attention in personal relationships. And that definitely isn't you. Even if you don't believe in any of that, it *feels* nicer when you walk into a

bedroom where the bed is made, the clothes put away, and there is a sense of order and harmony. This is the place you wind down. It is your retreat, your sanctuary and it is where your mind, your soul and your psyche get to rest and rejuvenate. It's your couple haven.

A good way to look at it is to show yourself and your relationship the respect you would extend to others. If you had a guest, you wouldn't usher them into a bedroom cluttered with discarded clothes, malodorous gym shoes, magazines, used glasses and cups would you? Treat yourself with the same courtesy. Most people are busy, and during the week your home can become a little messy. Just do your best to see the bedroom doesn't get that way. Take turns to make the bed in the morning; if you have a duvet or doona, this takes about ten seconds. Plump the pillows and if you have decorative cushions arrange them against your pillows. Discarded clothes from the night before should be either rehung or put in the laundry basket. Books or your Kindle should be placed neatly on your bedside table. Throw a kiss to the picture of the two of you that might be propped up on the bed stand and off you go.

Clutter in the rest of the house can happen by default. Merging two people's household items can create mess, and if storage space is limited even more so. Because of my husband's work we sometimes have to live in different states and the storage available in our temporary homes varies. If it's limited we go to a homewares store and buy storage helpers: plastic tubs, drawer organisers and shelving gizmos that double the available space in kitchen cupboards. We do this because clutter makes us cranky and we don't like being cranky. We get it sorted the first weekend we're there, so we can settle into our new home.

There is something relaxing about 'a place for everything and everything in its place' if you don't go overboard with it. It's just one less thing you have to think about, and it ensures petty tensions and frustrations don't arise between the two of you regarding small, inconsequential things. (This is particularly helpful if your partner is prone to the 'man-look'. The man-look is when he's looking for something and scans where he thinks it is without actually moving anything, then says he can't find it. You go and move one thing and there it is.)

Serenity now

Just like the clutter-busting techniques that help create a harmonious home, there are a couple of other things that can help keep your home a stress-free zone. Cordless headphones that connect to your television and sound system can be fantastic when the two of you are busy doing different things. They cost around AU$100 but if you're living in a smallish space they are worth every cent. Perhaps your partner is a fan of murder and mayhem movies but they give you nightmares for weeks. He puts on the headphones and you can sit quietly reading your book without having to listen to the gunfire and the screams. My husband's eye starts to twitch when, one after the other, I watch my two favourite shows about fashion stylists. So on go the headphones and everyone's happy.

The same thing goes for music. We generally have the same tastes, but sometimes one of us wants to listen to it loud while the other would prefer peace and quiet so the cordless headphones come in handy once again. It's consideration with the little things like this that help make living together a joy, and gadgets like these make this sort of consideration a lot easier.

Smells like home

Different scents can evoke memories of people and places. They can enhance your mood, relax and invigorate you. Scented candles, diffusers and oil burners can all give your home a softer, more relaxing vibe. Even some of the air fresheners available now have a much nicer fragrance than they used to. But if you really want to enhance the mood of your living space, essential oils are in a league of their own. They're natural mood enhancers and can be tailored to how you want to feel and the ambience you want to promote. You can even buy electric oil burners if you don't want to bother with tea lights. You might have some personal favourites and use them all the time. If not, or you've never used them before, here's a guide to the basic properties that relate to the different oils.

- **Balancing: rose, geranium, clary sage**
- **Energising: peppermint, citrus**
- **Meditation: sandalwood, frankincense, myrrh, cedar, juniper**
- **Passion: patchouli, ylang ylang, rose, jasmine, sweet orange**
- **Purifying: tea tree, eucalyptus**
- **Relaxing: lavender, chamomile, sweet marjoram.**

Sometimes the best way to choose the right oils is to go shopping with your partner and test them out, noticing which ones do the most for you. Often the shops that sell essential oils are an experience in themselves and a nice way to while away a Saturday afternoon.

Natural beauty

One of the best ways to relax at home is to have wide open windows and doors, letting lovely fresh air circulate. You can't beat it for renewing your living space and freshening things up. Obviously this isn't an option in subarctic temperatures or on a blisteringly hot day, but for the most part 'clearing the air' is as simple as opening up your home and letting it in.

Another way to improve the feel of your home is indoor plants. They don't have a scent, but plants generally induce a feeling of calm and relaxation. Apart from their calming appearance, some types of indoor plants improve air quality by removing toxins from the air. Then there's always the amazing scent of freshly cut flowers from the garden. And they're beautiful to look at as well.

A little *feng shui tip*: while everyone has their favourite plants here are a few points to consider. Cactus and plants with sharply pointed leaves are prickly and pointed like daggers, while plants such as peace lilies, lush indoor palms and ferns have soft, rounded leaves and give out a feeling of health and wellbeing. As you've probably guessed, *feng shui* recommends the latter.

Colour me happy

One of the things my husband and I are vigilant about is the presence of colour in our environment. In fact, I'd say he is more attendant to it than I am. Colour, like music, affects us immediately and deeply. Walk into a room painted black, then walk into a room with white walls and you will know what I mean. Most people, on entering a black room, can't wait to get out while white generally doesn't have that effect. Chromotherapy, or colour therapy, has been used since ancient Egyptian and

Chinese times to heal physical and mental ailments. There have been many studies done on the effect colour has on the brain – stimulating or soothing, increasing wellbeing or not. What has most definitely been established is that it does have recognisable, measurable and immediate effects on the brain and on brain functioning.

Think of the sayings 'I'm feeling blue', 'green with envy', 'seeing red'. It makes sense that the colours you use in your home will have a recognisable effect. Reds in the home are said to invoke passion and visual excitement in small doses. Too much red can incite feelings of agitation and anger, which is obviously something you and your true love can do without. Greens are calming, oranges vibrant and vital, while purples are luxurious and said to promote sexy time. But a bedroom full of purple might be a bit much. How you use colours in different spaces is a very personal thing. The most important thing is whether it makes you, as a couple, feel good.

Colour has long been seen as symbolic and evocative. Here are some generally agreed-upon meanings and effects. Just remember, some cultures have different interpretations and associated meanings of what a particular colour means.

White is symbolic of new beginnings and purity, and it has the big advantage of matching easily with all other colours. It promotes feelings of lightness and airiness, and is the perfect backdrop for stronger accent colours.

Black absorbs all other colours and is best used to accent and ground other colours. Generally the use of too much black creates an oppressive environment.

Red is a warm, stimulating and energetic colour. Too much, though, might create an overstimulated environment. Red is useful for appearing to increase the size of objects and for creating a feeling of energy, warmth and prosperity.

Orange is a vibrant colour encouraging communication, concentration and the intellect. According to the *feng shui* experts, too much can create a feeling of rebellion.

Yellow evokes feelings of optimism and decisiveness. It's often used in kitchens to promote entering the new day with a positive attitude.

Green is a calming, restful colour ideal for places where you relax – bathrooms, for instance.

Blue is said to create a peaceful and soothing vibe, although too much might make you feel sad and melancholy.

Purple is traditionally the colour of royalty and the first Roman emperors. It creates feelings of luxury, vitality and passion. *Feng shui* advises that purple is an ideal colour to evoke passion in the bedroom.

Pink is the traditional colour of romance and happiness.

Brown is great for creating earthy tones and grounding other colours and objects. Its positive effects are solidity and safety.

Recent scientific studies have shown that exposure to certain colours can have very positive effects but, like most things, too much of one thing can evoke negative feelings and energies. While the debate continues about whether colour has any lasting psychological effect, there is scientific evidence that initial exposure to a certain colour definitely affects a person's mood. As for the rest, you need to make up your own mind. Personal interpretation and taking note of personal preferences should always come first. As I talked about earlier, no-one can tell you how something makes you *feel*. A black room might make you feel as though you're skipping through a field of daisies. The colours that appeal to the two of you are known only to you.

It's the little things

Furnishings and decorative homewares can be a great way to add accents of colour without having to go all out and commit to a shade that may or may not work for the two of you. That way, you can change the vibe of a room with new cushions, a soft throw or a different rug. Colours like red, purple and orange are great in small doses, add visual excitement and can give you the positive psychological effects of a colour without any danger of an overdose. You can try a duvet cover, artwork or cushions or all of these with strong hues and see how you feel about them. Check with your furniture store whether they have a good returns policy. If they do, you can take something home and try it. If it doesn't work, you can ask for a refund or store voucher and try again.

For example, our dining room was an inoffensive palette of neutrals, a sea of cream and chrome. We found some amazing orange blown glass vases to give it some visual 'pop' but they didn't work as well as we'd thought. Something was still missing. It took us a few weeks to realise they needed grounding and we found an intricate black wooden slat table runner, which worked really well. We'd achieved the vibe we were going for. It just took a little longer than we'd thought.

Let there be light

Natural light is a favourite with most people, and if you're very lucky you have floor-to-ceiling windows and sliding doors to let those rays stream in. If you don't there are some very simple ways of maximising the natural light in your home. Choosing window treatments – shades, blinds, shutters, curtains and the like – that, when open, let in every inch of available light always helps, as does arranging furniture for the same effect.

Sometimes just moving a chest of drawers or a chair brings more light into the room and improves the feel significantly. No major expenditure required.

When it comes to not-so-natural light, the dimmer switch is brilliant for areas that need to serve a couple of different purposes. Work areas will tend to be more brightly lit, generating energy and vitality to support your toils and, more importantly, so you can see what you're doing! Your other areas, particularly your shared areas, give you the opportunity to create lighting that enhances how you feel together. Dimmer switches or a mixture of ordinary lighting and lamps allow the same areas to be bright and energising or subtle and restful depending on the time of day and what they're being used for. Soft lighting or candles at the end of the day can help you relax, allowing your brain to renew and recharge.

Visual prompts

You know how important the images, words and phrases you surround yourself with are to promote steering your mind down the right neural pathway when it comes to love. The unsingling process used the power of visual prompts to great effect. You used your treasure map and treasure app, and modified your living space to ensure it contained only positive visual cues regarding love. The journey now continues.

Visual prompts are still important. Once you've met your true love you'll want to make sure that your environment is sending out messages that are in alignment with *what the two of you want*. Let's extend what we've already done and consider these visual cues for the space you and your love now share:

- **Display happy photos of the two of you around your home. This is a no-brainer.**

- Create a new photo slideshow starring the two of you on your treasure app. This can include photos of the two of you interspersed with photos of places you want to go and things you want to do together. Have this playing in the background when you're home as a great reminder to focus attention on what you both want.
- Remember: you don't want magazines or books with negative love themes or titles strewn around the place. Keep the positive love neurons humming.
- Keep the energy moving. Things change. If you find some of your prompts are no longer giving you the same zing, find some that do. You might have fulfilled some of the things on your wishlist. If you've now visited the Grand Canyon, for example, include photos of the two of you there. And if you've come up with new adventures you want to experience, add those to your list.
- Visual prompts can be accidental. I bought my husband a mug for Valentine's Day that says 'Best Husband Ever!'. It's particularly cute and not quite as cheesy as it sounds. And now, every time my eyes light on it, it reminds me how lucky I am and how much I love him.
- Choose artwork that's 'up'. Beautiful scenes, lovers embracing, images of iconic places you want to visit together, magnificent abstract art. Whatever floats your boat, as long as it promotes feelings of happiness, togetherness, beauty or serenity.

You'll be amazed how simple things in your home can keep those neural pathways focused on the happy and the light. And you might be pleasantly surprised by how interested your true love is in keeping the unsingled vibe going. My husband's been on board from the get-go. I'm pretty sure by now you know what to do. Enjoy creating your harmonious home.

The end and the beginning

In this final step, you've come full circle. You modified your living environment with great success at the start of your unsingling journey, so it's appropriate that we end our time together here. True love has found its way to your door. Love is a mystery. No-one has ever managed to figure out the mathematical equation that makes two hearts blend seamlessly and I don't think they ever will. But believing in it has brought it to you, one of the best, most precious gifts life can give.

Congratulations! You've found someone amazing to spend your days and years with. Take care of each other, be kind to one another, have fun. And keep playing for Team Love!

Home is where the heart is checklist

♥ Sooner or later, moving in together is generally part of the true love experience. Whether or not you believe in *feng shui* there is enough evidence to show that a living space which reflects and generates positive energy will support you as a couple. You want to create a space that will promote harmony in your relationship and make you both feel good.

♥ Clutter-busting is pretty popular these days and the storage helpers available are substantially cheaper than they used to be. If, when you're merging your things together you find storage is limited, getting organised fast is the sanest approach and the best way to keep everyone smiling.

♥ Keeping your bedroom clutter free will keep you on the right side of the *feng shui* line. Treat yourselves as you would a guest. Even if the rest of the house gets a little messy during the week, keep your bedroom in the love zone – clean, clear and inviting.

♥ A great gadget that can do wonders for creating harmony in your home is cordless headphones linked to your entertainment unit. Perfect for when one of you feels like turning the music up loud and the other wants to relax and read a book, or when you want to watch something on TV that is of zero interest to your partner.

♥ Using essential oils is an easy way to enhance the ambience of your living space. Different oils promote different moods and you use them according to how you want to feel. Some of the stores that sell oils also sell lovely homewares, books and candles. Spending a lazy Saturday afternoon with your love pottering around stores like this, testing out what scents appeal to the two of you, can be romantic in itself.

♥ Fresh air, whenever and wherever possible, helps create a feeling of expansion and optimism. Indoor plants provide a calming vibe and can also improve the air quality. *Feng shui* advises against spiky looking plants because they're said to cause spiky behaviour, not something you two have to worry about but soft, rounded leaves are said to promote health and wellbeing. And who doesn't want that?

♥ Colour affects your mood, there's no doubt about it. Strong colours can really brighten up a place if you don't go overboard with them, and give you a little zing when you glance at them. Finding things you both love that introduce colour and style is a great bonding thing to do together. Shopping for home 'things' is a nice thing to do as a couple, starting your life together as an 'us'.

♥ Sometimes maximising the natural light available is as simple as moving furniture or pushing blinds and curtains right back. At day's end, if you or your love is stressed, dimmed lighting or candlelight with a relaxing essential oil burning can really change the feel of your home and take you and your beloved's heart rates down several notches.

♥ Visual prompts are still an easy way to keep your mind in the love zone now that you've unsingled yourself. Use your treasure app, treasure map, slideshows and beautiful art; bypass gossip mags and movies about train crash relationships. Have items around that make you feel the love when you look at them.

♥ Congratulations! You're officially unsingled. And if you keep giving love the attention and respect it deserves, Team Love will stay with you and see you through.

Appendix 1

The science behind *Unsingle*

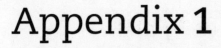

The power of neuroplasticity to transform the emotional brain opens up new worlds of possibility.
— Sharon Begley

Neuroplasticity refers to the brain's ability to rewire itself, changing your neural pathways based upon your experiences and what you give your focused attention to. My ten steps use the concept of neuroplasticity in relation to your feelings and your emotional life to support transforming long-held beliefs into something infinitely more positive when it comes to love.

This appendix will give you a simplified view of a neural pathway's components and the processes involved in rewiring the pathways in your brain. You'll read easy-to-understand sections on the following topics:

- **Your emotional brain**
- **Nuts and bolts of neuroplasticity**
- **'Using it or losing it'**
- **Tapping into love**
- **Imagination rewires your brain.**

So let's get started.

Your emotional brain

We know by now that neural pathways that are continually accessed develop and grow stronger, while those that are no longer used wither and decay. Author Sharon Begley, in her book *Train Your Mind to Change Your Brain*, talks of our emotions and our emotional brain as being under our conscious direction: ready, willing and able to follow our lead. She says:

> *We are not stuck with the brain we were born with but have the capacity to wilfully direct which functions will flower and which will wither, which moral capacities emerge and which do not, which emotions flourish and which are stilled.*

If, like many people, you've spent most of your life feeling as if your emotions run you, and that you have no control over them, this is great news. This knowledge opens up new possibilities if you are willing to take the time to direct your mind towards how you want to feel. Wilfully directing your focused attention determines which emotions flourish, and which emotions don't. Focusing on what you want and how you want to feel puts you in the driver's seat!

Nuts and bolts of neuroplasticity

So when did scientists discover the neuroplastic properties of the brain and uncover how the brain fired and wired and refired and rewired itself constantly throughout our lifetime? Like most scientific breakthroughs, significant signposts and extensive research paved the way. Here's a brief explanation of the end result to put you in the picture.

Breakthrough

Until the 1990s neuroscientists thought that from mid-childhood, the construction and behaviour of the brain were set and absolute. When it was discovered that this was not the case, an explosion of scientific inquiry began. Knowing that we weren't 'stuck with the brain we were born with' opened up a new world of possibility and saw the development of sophisticated neural imaging equipment. The scans obtained enabled scientists to study the behaviour of neural pathways in action; they discovered that the brain, far from being fixed, was constantly rewiring itself in response to stimulus. Thus the theory of neuroplasticity – a brain that changes its structure and function throughout life – became fact.

Remember the process mentioned in 'Step 1: Clearing the way': *focused attention stimulates neural firing, which creates new neural pathways.*

Now we're going to talk very simply but in a little more detail about the components and processes in the brain that make this happen.

The neuron

One of the basic building blocks of your nervous system is a neuron, a specialised type of cell which conducts electrochemical impulses. Neurons have receivers at one end, called dendrites, a word derived from the Greek word for tree, which gives a good description of what a neuron looks like. The dendrites are the receivers of the neuron and look like 'branches' of the cell body, while the axon of the cell is the 'trunk'. Stimulus is received through the dendrites and fires down the axon. At the end of the axon, the axon terminals (the 'roots') release neurotransmitters which transmit the fired impulse via the synapse to the dendrites of the next cell. The synapse is the small space between two neurons and it's how neurons link to one another.

Linked or interconnected neurons form neural pathways and linked or interconnected neural pathways form neural networks. If you change your neural pathways, your neural net begins to change.

What is neural firing?

Neural firing is the response of a neuron when it is stimulated. As we talked about in the description of the neuron, stimulus is received through the dendrites and *fires* down the axon. Then at the end of the axon, the axon terminals release neurotransmitters which transmit the fired impulse via the synapse to the dendrites of the next cell.

In simple terms, one neuron is stimulated. That neuron then releases neurotransmitters which flow through a synaptic connection to the dendrites of the next neuron and so on through a chain of neurons. The connected neurons form a neural pathway.

If you'd like a little more science ... The impulse coming in through the dendrites causes the movement of negatively charged particles (ions) into the cell via its axonal membrane and positively charged particles (ions) out via the same membrane. When this movement of ions into and out of the cell reaches a threshold level, an impulse (known as an action potential) is created, which fires down the axon to the axon terminals. The nervous system uses this neural firing to relay messages in the body. The release of neurotransmitters from the axon terminals of one neuron to the dendrites of the next neuron will cause that next neuron and subsequent neurons in the neural pathway to continue firing.

New neural pathways are formed when synaptic connections are made between a chain of previously unlinked neurons.

'Neurons that fire together, wire together'

These six simple words are known as Hebb's axiom. It means that if a set of neurons have fired together before, there is an increased likelihood they'll fire together in the future. Why is this important? As you continuously and repeatedly fire those 'love is good' pathways the connections between synapses grow stronger and you increase the likelihood of future firing. This is great neural news for unsinglers. Your neural pathways consistent with what you want grow stronger and your neural net – when it comes to love – is changed.

Putting it all together: changing your neural net

Putting this all together, we see how this neural process – neurons firing together and wiring together – is at the heart of the approaches and tools we've talked about in *Unsingle*.

Every experience a person has, including thoughts, sensations and feelings – any focused attention at all – is embedded in neurons that form neural pathways and eventually a neural net. The more a person experiences or focuses on these same thoughts, sensations and feelings, the stronger this net becomes.

For example, the more a person has thoughts and feelings of how wonderful love is, how real it is and how much fun feeling loved is, the more entrenched this belief will become. Their everyday life will be experienced through this new, improved neural net, which in turn supports the continued firing and wiring of this pathway.

Lack of use of the old 'love is pain' network and its replacement with a 'love is fun' network can mean long-held beliefs begin to dismantle themselves and become neural history. The neurons no longer fire together, therefore they no longer wire together. The longer the neural pathways are left unstimulated, the more complete the dissociation of the linked pathway becomes.

Using it or losing it

'Use it or lose it' is a commonly used phrase. In neuroscience, it refers to the fact that learning new behaviours and skills keeps your brain healthy, happy and buzzing. Just as we're all encouraged to exercise our bodies, neuroscientists, particularly since the discovery of neuroplasticity, tell us how important it is to keep things active in there by activities such as learning a new language and completing challenging crossword puzzles.

When it comes to unsingling I have a slightly different take on this phrase. Think of it like this …

Use it: You want to keep a neural pathway firing so you apply this premise. Continue to give your focused attention to what you want. Create games or processes, utilising things like your treasure app and 'acting as if' that encourage and stimulate these pathways and entrench these beliefs. Don't assume it will do this all by itself. Your mind and brain are awaiting your command, not the other way around. The more practised a belief or attitude becomes, the easier it will be for you to access it. Remember that.

Lose it: When you want to lose a neural pathway, apply this premise. Don't give it any of your focused attention. Disengage from any train of thought that isn't working for you when you become aware of it. Synaptic pruning occurs when unused synapses weaken. Eventually, the unused synapses are eliminated completely, leaving behind more efficient networks of neural connections or neural nets. These more efficient networks support what you want in your life.

'Losing it' is supported by activities mentioned in the unsingling steps 'Clearing the way', 'Flipping the switch' and 'Negativity diet'. These activities remove from your attention visual or mental prompts that could send you down the wrong neural pathway.

By 'using it' and 'losing it' appropriately you flip the switch, making the effort to move your mind and your brain in the direction you want it to head. This is the way you start to make your mind work for you.

Tapping into love

Sometimes 'losing it' is easier said than done. You know your mind isn't working for you, but you seem powerless to move beyond your fears and leave them behind. Your fight or flight response has become engaged and you are going for the ride.

What you need to do is change what's going on in your brain. Since this appendix is about science, let's concentrate on that. The limbic system has gotten a lot of attention lately within the neuroscientific community and this is where 'the ride' begins. The intensity of your feelings isn't fantasy, its physiological reality and you need a method or technique that will switch this response off. This is where the art and science of tapping comes in.

Tapping is a mix of modern psychology and ancient Chinese acupressure and has been scientifically proven to dramatically decrease stress hormone levels and disrupt and turn off the fight or flight response which hinders positive neural growth.

The fight or flight, or limbic, response, said to be one of the most overworked neurological processes in your body these days, is no longer activated by fear of death and dismemberment as per its evolutionary design. These days it is set off by not receiving five 'likes' to your latest post within five minutes, from fear of losing your job, fear of being too fat, too skinny, being alone, getting hurt, missing out, social death ... the list goes on. So what happens physiologically when this panicked feeling assails you and you feel frozen in place?

The alarm sounder and the records keeper

Let's go inside your midbrain for a minute and meet the alarm sounder (your amygdala) and the records keeper (the hippocampus). These are the guys you need to calm down, to let them know they can take a break and get out of the way while you're unsingling yourself. Assuaging them is one of the great unknown keys to positive neural change and retraining your brain for love.

The almond-shaped amygdala is a complex part of the brain essential for decoding emotions, and particularly stimuli that threaten us. Evolution has designed it so that many of our body's alarm circuits converge here. It receives several connections from its old friend, the hippocampus, which is responsible for memory storage and retrieval, and providing contextual associations. They work in tandem and together they are capable of great things e.g. saving your life. They're also capable of prompting 'two plus two equals five' emotional responses to external or internal stimuli. This is where things get a little sticky.

To understand how they operate let's imagine you have a new person in your life who doesn't call when he says he will. Your previous partner also never called when he said he would; he was deceitful and unreliable, a total nightmare. The silent phone triggers associations and mental leapfrogging where, within seconds, this new guy is the world's worst, intent on causing annihilation to your emotional landscape. Your heart is pumping, your adrenaline is coursing and you literally cannot sit still. You cry, you wail, you curse love and all who walk before her. Your mental agitation is off the Richter scale. When he calls to apologise and you find out his mother had been rushed to hospital and he'd left work to be with her forgetting his phone on his desk, you feel incredibly silly. You tortured yourself, exhausted yourself and wreaked havoc with your love zone for nothing.

This is the limbic response you want turned off.

So what went on there? When your phone didn't ring, your hippocampus and your amygdala smelt trouble and started messaging one another 'We need to check this out. Didn't we go through this before? Should we activate Defcon 1? We need to get onto it stat.' The clever hippocampus knows exactly where to go to retrieve the related memory and how to compare and ascertain the status. Within microseconds it brings up the old, embedded memory, evaluates the data and because of neural training and its contextual capabilities it reasons 'Yep! It's a threat all right. Same old, same old' and the new fellow gets lumped in with the old one, just like that. It tells the amygdala to set off the alarm (as you know, the more practised a feeling or emotion, the more readily the neural net is accessed and travelled down.) The barking frenzy begins, the sirens start wailing and off you go. You're 'using it' when what you really want to do is 'lose it' and you have strengthened neural pathways that you want – more than anything – gone.

The aim in unsingling is for your limbic response to get out of the way unless your actual physical survival is at threat. Even the thought of having this experience in the future can set this response in motion. Imagining you've met someone you're very interested in and projecting onto the future relationship the question 'How would I feel if he didn't call?' (which us girls have a tendency to do) can get this whole thing rolling. It is incredibly powerful and it can stop your unsingling in its tracks – for nothing!

Tapping quietens the fight or flight ride with remarkable ease and efficacy. When you tap through a sequence, detailed in 'Step 3: Flipping the switch', regarding what is bothering you and activate those meridians, you send a message to your amygdala and hippocampus that everything is all right and they can relax, trusting that it's going to be fine. The siren stays quiet, the pathways you want eliminated remain dormant and your mind continues playing for Team Love.

This is how tapping works its magic and allows you to calm down and facilitate neural change. It means that by the time you've completed your unsingling steps, your love zone will be in such magnificent shape that when your new person turns up, your reaction to a silent phone would be: 'Something must have happened. Hope everything's okay. I'm sure I'll hear from him soon.'

And if he's the right person for you, you will!

Imagination rewires your brain

Throughout this book I talk a lot about using your imagination. Interestingly, studies have been conducted which prove the effect of the imagination on the brain. Alvaro Pascual-Leone, a professor of neurology at Harvard Medical School, ran a study which showed that physically practising a skill and imagining practising a skill result in an almost identical restructuring of the neural pathways and the brain. The volunteers for the study were broken into two groups, with both groups learning a five-finger piano exercise. The first group practised playing the piano two hours a day for five consecutive days, while the second group only imagined they were playing the piano for the same time period. The second group's hands remained still while they imagined. Using neural imaging equipment, the researchers discovered something pretty amazing by the end of the week. In *both* groups of volunteers, the section of the brain devoted to the finger movements used to play the piano had increased substantially. As is evident from this study, imagination really does work.

Think about it, imagine it, picture it, sense it and your brain remodels itself to include the new-found belief or skill.

Now that you've had a brief look at neuroplasticity, you know more about what is going on behind the scenes as you unsingle yourself. You know more about the amazing ability of your mind to change your brain, and best of all you now know that you're in charge. Your love zone is under your control and yours alone. And for singles ready for their own happily ever after there isn't any much better news than that.

Appendix 2

Neural firing and love – studies of the heart

Over the last decade scientists seem to have become as obsessed with affairs of the heart as the rest of us. Neuroscientists have joined the ranks of poets, artists and playwrights, determined to give us the lowdown on love. It seems that every other week a new study emerges about the effects of love, long-term relationships and marriage on a person's health and mental wellbeing. Couples have been put to the test. Literally. Take a look.

Study 1: I wanna hold your hand

Neuroscientists wanted to study the protective effect of a good relationship on a person's mental and physical health and wellbeing. For unsinglers the results will give a nice confirmation that true love is worth the wait.

James Coan, an assistant professor of clinical psychology at the University of Virginia, was very surprised by the results of a hand-holding study he did in 2006. He and his team gathered a test group of sixteen happily married couples with the intention of examining the protective effect of a loving relationship on a person's psyche.

Each woman in the study agreed to be hooked up to an fMRI (functional magnetic resonance imaging) machine, which measures brain activity thereby allowing the researchers to observe the brain's response to stimulation. The chosen stimulation was a mild electric shock to the ankle to be administered three times. During the first shock the woman was alone; for the second she was holding the hand of a stranger; finally, each woman held her husband's hand during the third shock.

Monitoring the area of the brain related to the release of stress hormones, the results were pretty incredible. Coan said that even though they'd conducted the study expecting to see marked differences in how the women responded when holding their husbands' hands, even he and his team were surprised by the results.

The overall findings

The researchers did not anticipate the extent to which the quality of the relationship would affect the response (which had been assessed via the DAS method, a standardised assessment of relationship quality). All the relationships within the test group rated between medium and the highest possible 'happiness' levels. For all couples, when holding the hand of a spouse, the region of the brain responsible for processing potential threats – the fight or flight response – was significantly less active. Interestingly, those who rated at the highest levels and had the highest quality relationships showed the least activity. Coan likened this to the equivalent of taking a drug. He said that, from his study's findings, if a relationship was of high quality, the benefit the person received from hand-holding was 'better than anything'.

What Coan was referring to was that when you're with the one you love, your hypothalamus (your brain's hormone production centre) can release hormones targeted to rejuvenation and repair rather than combating stress. Which means your body's systems are able to do what they're designed for, supported and unimpaired. Your general immunity is maximised, hence the correlation between true love and better health. Yay, true love!

Study 2: Is romantic love more satisfying?

An interesting meta-analysis, conducted by academics Bianca Acevedo and Arthur Aron at Stony Brook University in the United States, focused on establishing whether romantic love could be sustained over a lifetime and whether it was associated with more satisfaction in the relationship. Just to be clear, I equate romantic love with what I call true love, throughout the book.

The meta-analysis (a study in which the results of many studies are correlated) consisted of a good-sized group – over 6000 individuals – and the researchers reviewed 25 studies to gather their data. They classified the relationships in each of the studies as romantic, passionate (romantic with obsession) or companion-like love and categorised them as long- or short-term. The short-term relationship studies were of 18- to 23-year-old college students with the average relationship lasting less than four years. The long-term relationship studies were of middle-aged couples who had been married for an average of ten years or more.

So what was the variation in the satisfaction scale between the three groups?

1. **Romantic love partners rated highly on the satisfaction scale in both short- and long-term relationships.**
2. **Passionate love partners were highly satisfied with their relationship in the short term, but not in the long term.**
3. **Companion-like love partners reported only moderate satisfaction in both short- and long-term relationships.**

The lead researcher, Bianca Acevedo, made the following distinction between romantic and passionate love: romantic love has all the great chemistry, connection and engagement of passionate love, without the obsessive element. She also said that the feeling that your partner was 'there for you' went a long way towards feelings of romantic love.

The overall findings

The results were conclusive. Romantic love was linked to the highest satisfaction overall. The results regarding whether true love could be sustained over a lifetime were also clear. Romantic love, where the couple continued to make an effort to connect and remain close, did not diminish over time. The physical aspect of their relationship also stayed strong. The researchers also remarked on a correlation they found between high satisfaction in a relationship leading to increased happiness and greater self-esteem. All ample justification to continue playing for Team Love, don't you think?

Study 3: Still 'madly in love' after all these years

The results of the previous study prompted a further, much smaller study by the same researchers, Acevedo and Aron. They wanted to investigate what was going on inside the brains of people who professed to still be madly in love after twenty or more years together. They did this by comparing their scans to young, 'madly in love' couples who'd been together less than a year. The results underpin my theory – that true love just gets better and better over the years.

I have to admit, this one is a bit of a personal favourite. Using fMRI equipment they scanned the brains of the seventeen long-term relationship participants while showing them photos of:

- **their partner's face**
- **a close friend**
- **a highly familiar person to whom they had no emotional attachment**
- **a person who was vaguely familiar, to whom they had no emotional attachment.**

They then compared them with brain scans of people who were shown photos of their beloved with whom they'd recently fallen in love. The results were surprisingly similar; however, there was one important difference.

Similarities

With both the new lovers and the long-term couples, when looking at an image of their loved one there was marked activity in the dopamine-rich areas which comprise the reward centre in the brain. (Dopamine is also promoted by eating chocolate and using cocaine. It's the 'feel good' neurotransmitter.) But *these* dopamine surges were all natural/naturally occurring love-highs.

Point of interest: the notion that the feeling of safety which comes with long-term love results in the invariable trade-off with passion and sexual attraction was nullified. These couples reported having sex an average of 2.2 times per week, from which the researchers took that sexual attraction and connection doesn't have to fade. Acevedo said, if a couple were willing to put in the work to remain connected in this way, a fulfilling sex life is well within reach for married couples.

Differences
The marked difference between the 'recently in love' and the 'long-termers' was noted in the areas associated with fear and anxiety. For the couples who had been together for a couple of decades, this area of the brain was very quiet. Just as the comments made in the previous study suggest, long-termers have all the great chemistry, connection and engagement of passionate love, without having to deal with things like intrusive thoughts when they're supposed to be otherwise focused, and feelings of pining and anxiety. In fact, the long termers showed quite the opposite – a sea of calm and an activation of opiate-rich sites related to pain relief and pleasure. Similar to the findings in the hand-holding experiment, a love that lasts calms you down and helps you to feel safe.

The overall findings
When the researchers assessed the brain scans of the long-term couples, they could see quite clearly that these people hadn't

exaggerated when they said they were still completely in love. They registered the highest possible scores in almost all categories when looking at a picture of their spouse, the categories being compassion, friendship, joy, pride, love, passion and sexual desire. The lowest score came in at around 90 per cent, which was still significantly higher than their response to any of the other test photos.

Even their closest friend didn't register as highly as their partner when it came to the area of the brain associated with friendship, which points to my theory that your true love is often your best friend.

In conclusion

I have to admit that while I was very interested in these studies, and loving the scientific verification, I wasn't surprised by the findings and conclusions. And I don't think most happily coupled up people would be either. The idea that being with the one you love is often where you find your most peaceful times isn't new. These studies prove what humans have inherently known since almost the beginning of time: that a happy relationship protects us. It reassures us. It soothes us, calms us and helps us feel safe. The minute we feel our love's touch or even see a picture of our partner's face, we're eased and more at peace. It proves that our inner drive, our longing for this kind of love isn't some crazy, romantic notion. There are neurons and peptides, amino acids and cell receptor sites that combine in an incredibly complex reaction as a result of our experiences and the people we have around us. And these reactions, when in a happy relationship with a person we love and trust, benefit us in ways we're just beginning to understand from a scientific viewpoint.

Glossary

The glossary is broken into two sections: an 'unsingle' glossary and a neuroscience glossary.

Unsingle glossary

'Acting as if'
a) Thinking through and sensing or visualising an imagined scenario, integrating it into your real-time experience.
b) Using a physical action to prompt your imagination.

Broken record
Repeating the same information or very generalised information about your relationship to people who like to cause trouble, to avoid misinterpretation and to maintain loyalty and trust.

Faith wobble
When doubts enter your mind and cause your faith to be shaken. The faith wobble is common when leaving behind old, negative beliefs and remapping your neural pathways to hold positive expectations. As much as possible, try to observe this process rather than participate.

Flipping the switch
Making the effort to move your mind and your brain in the direction you want it to head. This is the way you start to make your mind work for you, modifying your environment and what you give your focused attention to, utilising tapping and active imagining to rewire your love zone and retrain your brain for love.

Focused attention
Giving something your undivided attention for a period of time.
To concentrate on a subject, memory or event. Causes creation,
rewiring or strengthening of related neural pathways within
your brain.

Imagination
The formation of ideas, images or concepts of external objects
not present to the senses.

Love zone
Neural correlates and associated pathways related to romantic
love and relationships that form neural nets within your brain.
Previous experiences of love and relationships are recorded
and encoded within these neural nets, which in turn form your
belief system around love. All subsequent romantic experiences
will be seen through this filter, which is why you want to ensure
your neural correlates, when it comes to love, are predominantly
positive and reflect what you want.

Lunging
The practice of stepping one foot forward, simultaneously
executing a deep knee bend with a full extension of your back
leg while trying to keep a straight face and your balance, usually
performed with your hands on your hips for your partner's
amusement in the privacy of your home. (Make sure you warm
up first or you could injure yourself!)

Man-look
An incomplete search for an item, e.g. when your partner is
looking for something and scans where he thinks it is without
actually moving anything, then says he can't find it. You go and
move one thing and there it is.

Mood change
If it's from good (mood) to bad (mood), may indicate you are

thinking thoughts that aren't working for you, thus heading down the wrong neural pathway and strengthening the wrong neural net.

Negativity diet

The practice of eschewing any negative relationship input while in the process of unsingling oneself. This includes programs watched on television, movies seen, magazines purchased, books read, discussions taken part in and music listened to. If it doesn't support love and happiness, it doesn't get your attention.

Pain Highway

Thinking of and entertaining memories of painful past events, reliving them in the present, reinforcing negative neural pathways and possibly creating a self-fulfilling prophecy.

Playing for Team Love

Creating an environment around you that supports the presence and power of love and happy relationships. Focusing your thoughts and beliefs about love on the positive rather than the negative. Zeroing in on examples of love and loving behaviour, and knowing true love is for you.

Pollyanna

A person who is always optimistic and believes that only good things will happen.

Slow burner

A lovely, gradual realisation that this is the person for you, your true love, the One.

Tapping

Also known as EFT (emotional freedom technique) it is a mix of ancient Chinese acupressure and modern psychotherapy. Tapping uses the fleshy part of the fingertips to tap on designated acupressure meridian points (on the face and body) while verbalising thoughts or concerns. Scientifically proven to turn off the limbic/fight or flight response, which is one of the biggest blocks to positively rewiring and retraining the brain for love.

Thunderbolt

Love at first sight, an immediate soul connection.

Treasure map

A physical picture of your desired reality, usually a collage of images, photos, words and phrases that are personally meaningful to you and that invoke true love.

True love script

Taking a point from your 'yes please!' and 'no thanks!' list and expanding it into a script. The script details exactly how you would like the scenario to unfold, not holding back or restricting the details, and at the same time making it feel 'normal'.

Undershare

The practice of discretion regarding your relationship. Only sharing things about the two of you that you know your lovely man would be happy for others to know about. When in doubt, leave it out.

Unsingled

Having followed the ten unsingle steps you have met your one true love and are blissfully happy.

Visualisation

Formation of a visual image, a mental image that is similar to a visual perception.

'Yes please!' and 'no thanks!' list

A list of the things you want your true love relationship to embody, written in the present tense, as if it already is.

Neuroscience glossary

Amygdala
Almond-shaped section of the midbrain that is part of the limbic system. Contributes to emotional processing and to the formation of emotional memories. It is responsible for sending alarm signals that instigate the fight or flight response.

Axon
Long fibre of a neuron, which conducts an impulse away from a cell body.

Axon terminal
Occurs at the end of an axon, from which neurotransmitters are released to flow across the synapse to the next neuron.

Cell body
The central part of a neuron, containing its nucleus. It works to maintain healthy cell function.

Dendrite
The receptors of a neuron, branch-like in structure. They receive an impulse from the previous neuron via the synapse.

Fight or flight response
Response to stimuli, either external (e.g. a physical threat) or internal (e.g. negative memories or associations) originating in the limbic system within the midbrain, causing an increase in heart rate and blood pressure, adrenaline and blood sugar surges and muscle tension, preparing the body to defend or flee. Also known as the acute stress response or limbic response.

Functional magnetic resonance imaging (fMRI)
A procedure that detects changes in cerebral blood flow and in doing so measures the brain's activity. This technique relies on the fact that the brain's blood flow and neural firing are coupled.

When a particular area of the brain is in use, blood flow to that region increases.

Hebb's axiom

The expression 'Neurons that fire together, wire together'. If a set of neurons have fired together before, there is an increased likelihood they'll fire together in the future. Repeated firing strengthens neural pathways.

Hippocampus

The memory indexer within the limbic system. Processes and sends short-term memories to the appropriate hemisphere of the brain for long-term storage. Retrieves them when required. Provides contextual associations.

Hypothalamus

Has been called the command centre in the brain. Structure in the limbic system that coordinates hormone production and is pivotal to regulation of emotion and targeted repair. When the fight or flight response is activated it sends resources to fight threat instead of repair and restore.

Limbic system

A system of structures in the midbrain that control various bodily functions, including regulating hormones, interpreting emotions, feelings and responses, and memory storage and retrieval. It is where the fight or flight response originates. See 'Amygdala', 'Hippocampus' and 'Hypothalamus'.

Mind

The faculty of consciousness in a person, the awareness of thoughts, feelings and experiences.

Neural pathway

A set of linked or interconnected neurons. Strengthened by repeated use. Lack of use leads to dissociation of the neural pathway (neural pruning).

Neural (synaptic) pruning

The dissociation of neurons in a neural pathway, where the synapses no longer fire. This is related to the 'use it or lose it' premise. If you don't use it, you lose it.

Neural net

A set of linked or interconnected neural pathways. Formed in association with, for example, a learnt behaviour, motor skill or emotional response/state.

Neural correlates

Patterns of neural firing associated with thinking about a particular subject or a learnt skill (in unsingling, thinking or processing input on the subject of love and relationships).

Neural firing

The response of a neuron when stimulated. The stimulated neuron releases neurotransmitters from the axon terminals, which are transmitted via the synapse to the dendrites of the next neuron, stimulating it in turn.

Neuron

One of the basic building blocks of the nervous system, a specialised type of cell which conducts electrochemical impulses. It comprises dendrites (receivers) at one end, a cell body, and a long axon ending in axon terminals (transmitters).

Neuroplasticity

The ability of the brain to continuously rewire and reorganise itself (change neural pathway connections) based on the object of attention.

Neurotransmitters

Chemicals released at the ends of neurons (axon terminals) that diffuse across the synapse and activate the downstream neurons' receptors (dendrites).

Stimulation

An action, such as focusing attention, which initiates or increases neural activity.

Synapse

The small gap between neurons. An impulse is conducted across the synapse by neurotransmitters, released from the axon terminals of one neuron and received by the dendrites of the next neuron.

Use it or lose it

In this book, 'use it' is making a conscious effort to focus on what you want and continue activating the neural pathways you want strengthened. 'Lose it' is making a conscious effort to remove attention from what you no longer want to experience, therefore deactivating neural pathways you want gone.

References

Acevedo B. and Aron, A. 2009, 'Does a long-term relationship kill romantic love?' *Review of General Psychology*, American Psychological Association, vol. 13, no. 1, 59–65.

Acevedo B., Aron, A, Fisher, H. and Brown, L. 2011, 'Neural correlates of long-term intense romantic love', *Social Cognition and Affective Neuroscience*, doi: 10.1093/scan/nsq092.

Begley, S. 2007, *Train Your Mind to Change Your Brain*, Random House, New York.

Bradford Wilcox, W. and Dew, J. 2011, 'Give and you shall receive? Generosity, sacrifice and marital quality', National Marriage Project working paper no. 11–1, SSRN: http://ssrn.com/abstract=1970016 or http://dx.doi.org/10.2139/ssrn.1970016.

Coan, J.A., Davidson, R.J. and Schaefer, H.S. 2006, 'Lending a hand: Social regulation of the neural response to threat', *Psychological Science*, Dec; 17(12):1032–9.

Dispenza, J. 2008, *Evolve Your Brain: The science of changing your mind*, Health Communications Inc., Deerfield Beach, Florida.

Dispenza, J. 2012, *Breaking the Habit of Being Yourself*, Hay House, Carlsbad, California.

Doidge, N. 2010, *The Brain That Changes Itself*, Scribe Publications, Melbourne.

Emoto, M. 2004, *The Hidden Messages in Water*, Beyond Words Publishing, Hillsboro, Oregon.

Gawain, S. 1996, *Creative Visualisation*, New World Library, Novato, California.

Gilbert, E. 2010, *Committed*, Penguin Books, New York.

Hill, N. 1965, *The Master Key to Riches*, Fawcett Crest Books, New York.

Murphy, J. 1997, *The Power of Your Subconscious Mind*, Simon & Schuster, Sydney.

Ortner, N. 2013, *The Tapping Solution*, Hay House, Carlsbad, California.

Pascual-Leone, A. 2001, 'The brain that plays music and is changed by it', *Music and the Brain*, ed. R. Zatorre and I. Peretz, *New York Academy of Sciences*, Jun; 930:315–29.

Pert, C. 1999, *Molecules of Emotion: The science behind mind–body medicine*, Simon & Schuster, New York.

Terah Collins, K. 1996, *The Western Guide to Feng Shui*, Hay House, Carlsbad, California.

Recommended viewing

What the Bleep Do We Know!? DVD, directed by William Arntz, Betsy Chase, Mark Vicente, 2004.

The Tapping Solution DVD, created and produced by Nicolas Ortner, produced by Jessica Ortner, directed by Nicholas Ortizzi, 2011.

Any movies or television programs that make you laugh and/or feel good about love!

Acknowledgements

My utmost thanks to my reading group, in particular my beautiful sister Mary. You are one of the smartest, funniest babes I know. I don't know what I would have done without you. Anything I said about you guys would be an understatement. Thank you for loving *Unsingle* and for your support every step of the way. Thank you, thank you, thank you.

To Sean Doyle and the team at Lynk Manuscript Assessment Service, thank you for providing a brilliant service, for the encouragement, the professional feedback and for getting *Unsingle* where it needed to go – namely to Finch's front door.

Speaking of Finch Publishing, what an amazing group of people. To Sam and Laura, thank you so much for helping a new author find her way. Your kindness, support and professionalism have been very much appreciated. To Rex Finch, thank you for giving my book the go-ahead. *Unsingle's* found a very happy home.

I've always wondered about the acknowledgements in other books and the author's extreme gratitude to their editors. I no longer wonder. Karen, you are amazing.

To my other beautiful sister, Angie. You are a special soul. I must have been very good in a past life to deserve two sisters like you and Mary. Thank you both for your support, your insight and your love. Blessed am I to have the two of you in my life. And to my nephew Sam, for helping me out when I needed you. I love you very much.

I'd also like to thank Dr Joe Dispenza, the person who started me on this journey. Your discussion on the law of associative memory and neural nets in relation to love in the movie *What The Bleep Do We Know* woke me up, and I will be forever grateful. They say when the student is ready, the teacher will come. The student was ready and the teacher did come. Thank you, thank you, thank you.

And finally to my husband Dave, the love of my life. You are kind and warm and I love you more than words can say. Thank you for making me laugh and for making my unsingling such a success. And most importantly, thank you for loving me in the way I've always wanted to be loved.